Thomas Edgar McNally has forever expressed himself to the world through a heart filled with love and gratitude and a spirit of belief in what's possible for all. He meets and receives each person right where they are on their journey, advocates for what's best for others, lives to serve and strives to unlock the doors, provide the programs or light the path to solutions for their better health and greater well-being. McNally takes the reader back in time, his special skill as an author, music composer, mental health specialist and storyteller radiates his talent of capturing the journey through the 1950s and 1960s.

To my buddy, friend, CRO, Golden Bear and American Hero: Gary.

RIP

Arlington National Cemetery

Arlington, Virginia, USA

Thomas Edgar McNally

CRO'67 A GOLDEN BEAR STORY

A Coming of Age Memoir of The 50s and 60s

AUSTIN MACAULEY PUBLISHERS®

LONDON · CAMBRIDGE · NEW YORK · SHARJAH

Ordering Information
Quantity sales: Special discounts are available on quantity purchases by corporations, associations, and others. For details, contact the publisher at the address below.

Publisher's Cataloging-in-Publication data
McNally, Thomas Edgar
CRO '67 A Golden Bear Story

ISBN 9798891559233 (Paperback)
ISBN 9798891559240 (Hardback)
ISBN 9798891559264 (ePub e-book)
ISBN 9798891559257 (Audiobook)

Library of Congress Control Number: 2024917003

www.austinmacauley.com/us

First Published 2024
Austin Macauley Publishers LLC
40 Wall Street, 33rd Floor, Suite 3302
New York, NY 10005
USA

mail-usa@austinmacauley.com
+1 (646) 5125767

To Taz, my soulmate, who tolerates me and encourages me to pursue music and writing. A truly blessed partnership! A once in lifetime soulmate!

Lester, my agent, friend, inspiration, fiancé and SILLY, SASSY, SEXY, SMALL, and SMART SOULMATE!

Jon, my lifelong best buddy, friend, and very much part of the trifecta of crazy, during the height of the Jon, Thom, Gary 1960s…Together, in partnership with our lovers, we share and create stories…CRO'67!

Table of Contents

Here and now…Introduction, Foreword as the story is told…

Sitting comfortably at home, bathrobe, coffee and the lingering afterglow following another round of great sex—no, passionate loving with my fiancé. Wow, was I lucky, and the weekends were starting to become weeks!

"Get this, TAZ, an email inviting us to a huge, 'getting 70' party down in Columbus. Guess it's time for us 'maturing' Golden Bears to gather together, celebrate one more time and see who's left standing!"

"So, what, handicapped parking for one and all?" exclaimed TAZ as she sauntered by, Arnold Palmer in hand, headed for the couch. "And no! This is your invite. I wasn't even a thought in my parents' brain or loins in the late 1960s. So, what's up with you seniors? Give me more details!"

"Well, it seems that over the 4th, when historically, all of the Upper Arlington folks celebrate their whiteness, there's going to be a hoedown at one of my classmate's high-octane Kentucky Derby kinda ranch, south of Columbus. It would be a fun time to just introduce you to so many of my childhood and high school chums."

"Sure, those who are still alive!" exclaimed TAZ. "Let me guess, Vietnam, drugs and too much self-entitlement most likely killed off the best of the lot."

"Honestly…Yup! You already know of a few…"

"Absolutely!" shrieked TAZ.

"Your very best friend, the fella who was married to that hamburger lady, who totally tanked on cocaine…"

"Yes, I know the stories. They seem to be endless," exclaimed TAZ, as she laid sprawled on the leather sofa, watching Blacklist.

"Well, others must know of this evolving get-together. I also see that two of my Columbus cousins are reaching out. I'll wait till later to read their emails. More than enough time for another round with you!"

"So, wait a minute. We're supposed to be headed to Dublin, IR to see Billy Joel and then off to see Roger Federer win Wimbledon?"

"You want to tank on these bucket list adventures to go smell horse poop and possibly the leaking Depends of your former buddies, out of whom many have already died and don't even know it as of yet?" TAZ quipped. "Also, I don't think that I am up to trying to explain to your brain-dead classmates that I do not have daddy issues," TAZ exclaimed.

"Yes, you do…" I added.

"I wouldn't even consider this short road trip if it wasn't for the pending legal issues I have with those who recently were discovered to have been skimming from me for the past 4 years. Plus, you have legal emancipation and guardian issues that must be resolved with your oldest before August. So, rethinking being out of the country for more than a month may be the order of the day, just saying."

"I seriously need to try and recapture that lost income or get a business loss deduction. However, I need to visibly demonstrate that I have gone after the slime balls who have stolen from me. So, time is of the essence for me and you!"

"Fine! How about you come over here and we talk about what you want to eat for breakfast…" TAZ exclaimed as she rolled onto her back and undid her robe…

Days and weeks passed. Nothing has been decided, so I roll out a "possible." "So, TAZ, what'cha think? Spring turkey hunting and trout fishing are approaching quickly. I was thinking of inviting up a bunch of my childhood and high school friends to the lodge for a 'fin and feather' extended weekend. We could get caught up, plus, I can determine if this horse ranch classmates party is worth attending. Plus, I have concerns that have been expressed to me from my Columbus cousins."

"Like what?" spouted TAZ.

"By their accounts, someone seems to be stalking me on Ancestry. I guess there have been connection requests that all center on me."

Weeks passed, and then via an older sibling, I learned that there was a fella who was 'backdooring' the family, saying that I was his father! Ancestry was indicating that there was a high probability. This guy was born and adopted in 1969. My first thought was no way. I was living in California.

A weekend rendezvous with TAZ was approaching, and it was time to spill the proverbial beans. She needed to know. Otherwise, this could blow up in my face and I could lose the love of my life!

Well, we had a five-day road trip planned, headed to the dock condo, antique shops, casino and the land of the Amish. Over a steak and $250 bottle of red wine at the casino steakhouse, I broke the news. TAZ's response was precious! However, she asked for another glass of her favorite wine!

"Seriously! You have a fucking kid who is older than me! You are such a whore! I have always wondered if you had kids all over the country. You and your lame friends were the Johnny Apple Seeds of sperm!" TAZ exclaimed.

"Since abortion was illegal then, this was literally an arranged union between an adoptive couple and a young lady who probably had no idea how she might have gotten pregnant."

"I have done the math, and since I was enrolled in college and lived in Columbus, I can only put myself in West Michigan during the last two weeks of November 1968. My three buddies and I, from Columbus, headed to the north woods of Michigan to try out deer hunting. We knew absolutely nothing. We just understood it was all about beer drinking and camping, so why not? Possibly some sort of parking lot rendezvous with a cute bar patron."

"Dang, it was the 60s. Chicago 7, Free Love, hippy chicks. I still had long curly hair, played in a band and was fit as hell. However, having a damn sexy girlfriend from Columbus, who was attending school in Athens, OH. No way would I have screwed any random chic. That would never have happened!"

"Maybe not! However, you dumbass. But dropping a load on some furry pussy, who later got shanked again, maybe by multiple others, let alone a boyfriend. Your sperm obviously won the race. Unless this is your older brother in action," offered up TAZ.

"Very doubtful!" I responded. "My brother was headed to West Michigan but that was definitely not his style. This is not a 100% done deal. That lawyer dude, who got OJ off, would probably say there is more than enough data that I am not this dude's bio father. The fact is, since birth, he has parents. Plus, he has an adopted younger sister. I have checked."

"Well frankly, my aged stud muffin, how you can remember anything from 52 years ago really amazes me!" TAZ was quick to add.

"Well, time for some invitations. Your little 'fin and feather' at the lodge rendezvous with your childhood, high school and college chums may just shed some light on all of this. Plus, your iconic Pleasantville, Wally and the Beaver, The Help and Nelsons upbringing should be a journey down memory lane, while all of you can still think clearly! Holy shit, look who the hell lived in just your neighborhood."

"I'm not too sure who that Woody football coach was, but I remember my dad always referring to him as a clown who hit an opposing football player during a game."

"You were his paperboy! Not to mention you went to high school not only with 'the lights aren't twinkling' gal, but also three grandkids of the richest man on the planet. Rather impressive if I do say so…" exclaimed TAZ. "Now, before these invites, get over here and let's get frisky."

"Why not! I am getting fucked in my ass by those stealing from me. My chances to see Federer fucking win at Wimbledon are now 'somewhere in the future'. And my chances for a life commitment to each other in the vestibule at St. Patrick's in Dublin have gone the way of seeing Piano Man on the shores of the English Channel. Why not, this ought to spice up our weekend!"

"Just so you know, I kinda like this daddy thang!" quipped TAZ. "Hey, do well and I just might keep you around, because there is no other classy lady on this planet who wants a whore like you…lol. Don't forget, I can easily afford, just with my lunch money, a bus load of Chippendales, so don't be kind! Just love me, you clown!" expressed TAZ.

The invitations were extended. Phone calls made. Sad news came back quickly that my childhood and high school chum, Gary, had died. Very difficult to wrap my brain around that reality. He was the ultimate stud. Kinda the Dolph Lundgren type. A beyond talented swimmer. He and I used to fish in the Scioto River, below Griggs Dam almost daily.

Gary, David and Bruce all headed my way following my parents who had pulled out of Upper Arlington and headed to West Michigan. Each had their own reasons for getting out of town that I learned about long after our adventure to Pines Point Federal Forest outside White Cloud, Michigan for the 1968 deer season.

Gary was under investigation for trafficking marijuana coming out of Vietnam. David was under some sort of surveillance for activities related to the SDS and the riots at the Democratic convention in Chicago. Bruce wanted a vacation and out of the spotlight of his father, a respected physician, who was under investigation for running abortion clinics in central Ohio. Me? I just wanted to try out a healthy high in the wilderness state of Michigan. We were all entitled white boys from the city. Beer drinking was our pastime and hanging out and bullshitting was our culture. Dang, we all had to borrow firearms and hunting clothing to actually pull this adventure off.

I shared with TAZ the reality of the upcoming visits. She was like, "Let me know when it's over!" However, she did bring up an important aspect of the social dynamics of Upper Arlington, the Golden Bears and some sort of lame bird name.

"Weren't you in a gang?" She expressed.

"Yup, kinda."

"Sure, it had some stupid bird name. I have seen your reunion shirts that have a bird with a cigarette, beer and sick ass expression. What the fuck is that all about?" TAZ inquired. "What were you guys, the Peckers? Or was your gang all about flying fucks, or what?" she added.

"Well, it was CRO. We were CRO 1967. It was more or less a party organization dedicated to endless partying. However, surrounding areas like the Short North, North High and Grandview wanted us to be like the Sharks and Jets from West Side Story. Maybe, but not really. CRO was an acronym for a saying and the girls' organization was ORC. Kinda like words in a mirror."

"So, what the fuck could CRO or ORC possibly mean? It makes no fucking sense," inquired TAZ.

"Well, to be honest but not gross, CRO means COCKS REACH OUT and ORC is OPEN and READY for COCKS! Hence, CRO and ORC."

"Seriously?" exclaimed TAZ.

"Yup, there is no turning back. This was the 60s and shit prevailed. The crow, or CRO, became the natural mascot." At one time, it was considered just to run with the school's logo of Golden Bears. A polar bear was actually in the hallway at school that was kinda golden, so that was the mascot. However, Jack Nickolas, the famous golfer who went to Upper Arlington was always referred to as the Golden Bear, because of his size and the color of his hair. Plus, he owned a grocery store named Golden Bear. It was obvious he would trademark the name. Plus, I'm sure it was a stretch to come up with a classy saying like COCKS REACH OUT, from the word GOLDEN or BEAR!

"Suffice to say, you CRO types were only concerned about where your peckers would end up. Own it!" TAZ exclaimed. "Sounds so very *fowl* to me…" TAZ just shook her head and laughed. Only in the land of the rich, famous and wannabes could one possibly find something so very lame. She added, "You know, you 3.2 beer-brain-dead chumps were tripping over yourselves to get noticed. Seriously, CRO and ORC? Let me guess, you were not smart enough to be the one who made, designed and sold the Ts and sweatshirts?"

"Nope," I exclaimed. "See, that's exactly why I am in the Fortune 500, and you are lucky to get random certificates of honor for saving the world…lol!" TAZ just strutted away, looking back long enough to say, "Follow me for some fun, whore!"

"Now?" I responded.

"Hell yes! There'll never be a better time. You and your chums will only talk pussy, parties and woulda shoulda's…" TAZ added. "So, besides loving me endlessly this weekend, enlighten me to the dynamics of the Golden Bears, Upper Arlington and CRO 1967," TAZ said as she rolled over to face me in the bed, butt naked and ready to snuggle.

"Fine!" I exclaimed. "It all starts when my dad proceeded with building a new home during the year I was born. He had bought a lot in Upper Arlington, Ohio. A community, new, but with a vision. Home to old money. We were the middle, and then eventually, the new money would define the suburb. At the time, the 50s and 60s, it was the land of gentry. Our time was a Camelot. The culture was unique, and now, all of the dynamics of the culture are almost surreal. It was a Once Upon a Time…I threw into the mix for comment."

"Okay, lover boy. Give me a reference or something that can put this 'Once Upon a Time' thang into perspective." TAZ exclaimed.

"Well, that's perfect! 'Once Upon a Time in Hollywood', you've seen. I was there, literally. So, let's use that as a reference and work backward. Kinda headed toward Wally and the Beaver, The Nelsons, and even Dennis the Menace. You've seen Pleasantville. Very much the same, but instead of the bowling alley, it was a classy country club. West Side Story, during its debut, was basically during the onset of our hormones and the desire to take on the world. It's a story of a time, place, people and things that no longer exist. Sure, all that remains are the faces and names, but the culture is tainted by reconstituted families, no moms at home. The evolution of technology and the world turning into fat asses," I gracefully added.

"Well, you have me, babe. 100 pounds of TAZ she-devil, so amp up and get on with it. I'm horny and this better have a satisfying ending. I also have six seasons of Blacklist to watch!" TAZ declared and stared into my very soul. "So, entertain and enlighten me with your CRO pecker stories…Let it begin, a Golden Bears story: CRO '67."

It took forty years for me to finally realize that my journey through life as an Upper Arlington Golden Bear transcended unique. This was the time and place where moms played bridge, and moms never working. Dads 'went to the office' and were home by 5:00 p.m. for 'martini time'. One could walk to any place one wanted to. Fresh bread smelled up your house three times per week. Ed, the milkman, dropped off milk, eggs, cheese, and cottage cheese neatly placed in the garage. The Tom Tarpy Grocery Store delivered our groceries. The Inhalator Squad was what the ambulances were called. All candy bars were 5 cents. The raunchiest things on TV stations were Soupy Sales and his banana cream jokes, and a random sexual innuendo from Jack Benny or Bob Hope! I don't think that Eddie really asked Mrs. Cleaver, "How was the Beaver?"

Our families had domestic help who did most of the household chores like ironing, washing, housecleaning and even cooking. These ladies were referred to as 'colored', which was the vernacular of the times for African Americans. Edna, our primary helper, had a long history with the McNally clan. She initially worked for my father's family of ten kids: Grandmother Susie aka Margaret Sullivan-McNally and Joseph McNally. She was a peaceful person, never raising her voice and who had high expectations of us kids. There were times when we thought of her as our mother, mostly because she was always present while my mom was out playing bridge and gossiping. Thinking of how Arlington was really got me to be pensive about my life; how I was raised and basically how, even though it was ideal, there was a social handicap that took years to try and shake free from, if you could ever get over it. Far too many stayed immersed in the Golden Bear Arlington notion, and many perished because of it. Success does not always breed success.

The overall social structure was unnatural by today's social dynamics. Dads worked, moms stayed at home. We all had one, some two, cars. No divorces, no domestic violence cases that you could hear in the night, no barking dogs. Cocktail hour always at 5, fried chicken on Sundays, and most ordered their clothes through the Sears, Lazarus or Union catalogs. Your orders were promptly delivered right to the front door. Calls were made on a landline. Ours, 458–0309 or Hudson, 80309. There were no area codes.

For our parents and for us aspiring youngsters, the social pecking order broke down to 'old' Arlington, 'middle' Arlington and 'new' Arlington. It was kinda like 'old money', 'some money' and 'very-new-but-we-have-a-lot money'. No matter how you bracketed it, most were doing well, way above the rest of the American world, but what tied everyone together was the link with the Golden Bears. Heck, even Jack Nicklaus, a graduate, took the Golden Bear logo with him as he moved into the bigger world.

My dad and family were in the lumber business. Dad could see the 'Upper Arlington' vision well, so in 1950, he purchased a lot of what was then the furthest northern boundary of Upper Arlington and proceeded with building a nice four-bedroom colonial home. Aerial photos of the construction site showed nothing more than a dirt drive. It was a very smart move, especially for the son of an Irish immigrant who had served four years in WWII and returned a decorated officer.

Upper Arlington prospered and grew at a phenomenal rate. Soon, parks, stores, police stations, fire departments, athletic fields, and churches popped up everywhere.

My mother was the perfect Golden Bear spouse. She was born in New Orleans and eventually raised in St. Louis, Missouri. She attended the University of Missouri, and besides being the Homecoming Beauty Queen, she earned a degree in business administration, which was quite an accomplishment for a lady in the 1940s.

That notion, or "Where did all of this start?" is what got me going in response to this pending reunion. The Golden Bears of Upper Arlington were again out to make their point that 'we are the best, the brightest, the toughest and most successful' people on this earth.

Back in the late 50s, the threat of war hovering over us each and every day, Upper Arlington had an answer to this. I believe it was a Sunday afternoon, and it was at the north end of the St. Agatha property. They, whoever they were, had the notion of exploding 25 lbs. of T.N.T. as part of an evacuation activity for the public. Well, what was lacking was realism, because we're talking about families who daily had to deal with the sonic booms of the jets parading by from the Wright-Patterson Airforce base. However, Civil Defense Alarms went off at exactly 12:00 noon each and every Friday! No, not tornado drills, war drills!

Well, what the whole event turned out to be was 'martini time' in the front yards of hundreds of homes. Kids were playing in the streets, parents were sucking vodka and gin, and a whole lot of what appeared to be weekend soldiers scrambling about to make this 'war-worthy'.

Earlier, my brother and a couple of friends had snuck into the woods behind St. Agatha to gather as much porn that was discarded as we could before the big boom. We wanted to save the stuff, but we weren't really sure where we were going to store it. Porn back then was natural little ladies baring their breasts. Nothing else, just tits, but enough exposure to help get a rise out of any lad. We figured that the parish priests were the source of these magazines. However, considering this was a convent housing twenty nuns, maybe it was theirs.

Well, 5:00 p.m. came around, and off went the explosion. Damn, it was one heck of a boom! I just thought to myself, *why?*

Moving Forward 5th Reunion

Well, as we got closer to the first reunion, I made up my mind that this one I would skip. I felt a sense of relief when I made that decision. I had been so socially tied to always join in with what the crowd did, but now I was thinking for myself. I had come to a point of self-actualization that I no longer needed the Golden Bear façade or image to protect me, honor me, or guide me. My thinking was now more grounded in reality, or so I thought!

I had made some nice reconnections with past friends, classmates and true buddies, but I just didn't see what this reunion had to offer. As I continued to receive emails, some with photos of guys and gals who I had grown up with, I realized that what was would never exist again. The glamour, the gang status, the feel-good fucks, the keggers and so much more were gone. There were some, though, that still wanted to relive some of our greatest days at the reunion. We all wanted to stay in 'Neverland', but Peter Pan had to grow up.

Most of the guys, or so it seemed, played in one rock band or another. I played for several, and I still play, but now, it's for pure enjoyment. However, my skills have improved tenfold. Well, someone on the reunion committee thought that it would be cool to reunite a composite band of musicians who would be willing to do some of the songs of our era. It had a certain Blues Brothers quality to it, but it did sound like fun. Playing Gloria, Satisfaction, Not Fade Away, and Dirty Water, doing the opening act for Bobby Seger and the Last Herd at the Sugar Shack and Herman and the Hermits at the Ohio State Fair. Plus, playing at the Columbus International Airport for Ted Kennedy, soon after Bobby was assassinated, we did the song "He was a Friend of Mine," written and recorded by The Byrds, who we later joined in concert at the ARC. As a matter of fact, I still have McGwinn's tambourine from that gig.

There was no way that this 'Blues Brothers' mentality of 'bringing back the band' was going to fly. So, I decided to pass and say *hasta la vista* to the whole shindig. I came to the realization that being in high school, the experiences, growing pains, the need to belong and be recognized was like being in the middle of an hourglass—stuck in that little pinch point and trying to maintain a demeanor that everything was cool, when in reality, for most, once it passed, we were all pretty glad that it was over. It becomes a relief when all of a sudden, you don't have to worry about sitting next to the 'wrong' classmate at lunch. Or even having a seat extended to you. The heaviest thing any student ever carries is their lunch tray.

There were other variables that influenced my thinking. Who wants to go revisit old times with former lovers, whom you had great sex with by the light of the dashboard lights and who now look like their mothers did back in the late 60s? Many of the 'in-crowd chicks' were sun goddesses and now looked like prunes. Plus, there was the pervasive risk of running into a drunken jealous boyfriend or husband who now wanted to show the world that they thought they could kick your ass. Being one who loved to invite trouble into my life, that possibility was very real.

My story lies behind the evolution of a society that prepares the young with goals, aspirations and wishes. However, the superficiality of the people within the society—that was basically under the vacuum of protection because of the denial of the residents. The key players who ran the system, and those who were most invested in winning at all costs, were not willing to self-examine that behind this Pleasantville façade were deep social and personal troubles for some. Any and all references to people, places, things, behaviors, actions or outcomes are purely coincidental. Well, the best place to start is always at the beginning. So, as this Golden Bear adventure truly unfolds, it is best to go back to the times of the heyday. The 1960s were when the Golden Bears were at their strongest—we had a high school with only three grades, which housed over 2000 pupils, two major junior highs and a bunch of elementary schools. Each geographic section of the Upper Arlington expanse had schools, libraries, swimming pools, parks, athletic fields, stores, police/fire stations, churches, and at one end the Scioto Country Club, and on the other, the OSU Golf Course.

This Normal Rockwell-like community had all of the fixings for not only ownership of many fine houses and estates but also numerous recreational facilities and libraries to keep everyone involved. The Scioto River was basically the west boundary, and mansions that adorned the shoreline along Route 33 were legendary.

During the heyday, there were no cellphones, computers, or iPods. We all learned to talk by using the phone. We learned to write because it was expected, and it was how you communicated with your girlfriend. We learned to remember by having to memorize numerous pages out of the dictionary as a form of punishment issued by one of the many sadistic nuns who taught us at St. Agatha. The St. Agatha Church and School was at the very hub of the Upper Arlington. Historically strong families sent their kids to this Grade 1–8 institution.

Sisters of Charity were primary proctors in the school, while a few lay teachers sprinkled through the grades. Our coaches were a bunch of wannabes who still thought they were 'superstars', but the reality was, most of them were 'have-been' or 'never-were'. They were kinda like Shane Falco with a bad attitude. Falco aka Keanu Reeves in The Replacements was a polished stud, but he had never found his niche.

The Fledgling

Kindergarten was the initial training ground to begin to fortify one as an aspiring Golden Bear. I attended Tremont Elementary, which was a public school that was slowly evolving as a show place for central Arlington. A swimming pool was under construction and so were many athletic fields including tennis courts and shuffleboard. I was lucky enough to be assigned to an 'a.m.' session of kindergarten. I was paired up with several other kids in the neighborhood to walk across the northern part to the school. I was much more interested in the construction of the pool.

Well, shit hit the fan when, about a week or so into the school year, Ms. Rink decided to call my mother to locate me. My mom had no excuses and no idea as to where I was. She and a few concerned moms set out to find this lost little 5-year-old. Of course, in that era, no one would have thought that some deranged sexual pervert might have your kid. Everyone always looked at each situation as one that was going to have a happy ending. Then my nanny hunted me down, and the silly part of all this was, the construction workers related to my mom that they had been paying me each day to go home. However, I just kept coming back, so I guess that I banked ten, fifteen or twenty bucks for watching the ways to put together a public pool. Cool!

Well, I returned to kindergarten, but I just wasn't with the routine. Frankly, I didn't have a clue as to what they were up to, but at least I knew my colors. I was also quite musical and liked to sing and dance. The expectations of kindergarten in those days were based upon socializing the student as opposed to trying to get them ready for Odyssey of the Mind. We learned to work in groups and look out for each other. The few kids that I met, which I liked, were invited to my spring birthday party.

I remember being quite anxious about having friends over. Many classmates headed to my house on a sunny Saturday to help me turn 6. We had fun, and interestingly, I would end up knowing these guys for all of my teenage years. However, one whose name I can't remember, failed in kindergarten, and so, he had moved back in his grade placement. What a painful thing to have to do to any child. Over the years, I would witness this same scenario many times over, and it always produced the same outcome: a kid who hated school, who started to develop some antisocial tendencies and a kid who would continue to struggle with learning to read. Forcing kids to be normal does not always work; in fact, it backfires.

As the kindergarten year slowly came to an end, it was time to start talking about where I was going for 1st grade. I really didn't have any say in it, but I remember that it worried me. St. Agatha's School was directly across the street from us, and since my parents were die-hard Catholics, it was obvious where I was headed. My dad had been in the seminary, and both of my parents had attended Catholic school through 8th grade. It was only logical that I followed their path. My older brother was already attending, so it was natural that that was where I would land in the fall.

Social anxiety is the nemesis of all students, and I was no exception. I had worries about using the bathroom, pissing my pants in class, and puking anywhere in the school. I was also quite conscious about that I wore to school, since Arlington, as a society, had certain expectations as to how you were supposed to dress and eat.

Well, all of my fears that I had about school came to reality, but luckily for me, they happened to other students. One that I hadn't thought of was a student shitting their pants in class. Yes, it did happen, and it was enough to make anyone sick. The nun in charge retrieved ammonia water and many rags and proceeded to wash the boy's desk. He apparently was sent home, but the stench was unbearable. I doubt if I ate lunch that day, and I can't even remember if that boy ever returned to class. I felt sorry for him. It was like the worst. We were all expected to stay seated in the classroom as the nun bathed his desk, she maintained this derogatory social commentary as she went about disinfecting his seat and desk. She was making this a social problem for this kid, and never once did she vocalize how physical illness can cause bathroom-type accidents. How totally lame.

As the years progressed, I would soon learn that it gets worse, kinda like in the movie Carrie, when she starts her menses in the locker room, and how the other girls just bury her in Kotex and other sanitary napkins. I do remember the many occasions of girls, as we stood to recite prayers prior to recess or lunch, who would have a blood spot on their bottom, about the size of an orange. Since the girls wore dark-green uniforms, it wasn't always clear what the spot was, but after the word got out from those behind the menstruating youngster, it was very clear that they were pumping blood from their virgin vaginas. What a sad embarrassment, because soon, you would hear they were whores.

Evolving sexually can't be an easy task for anyone. Our curiosity was always peaked by any flash of a forbidden part, a rumor of whose older brother or sister was 'doing it', or a peek at a 'dirty magazine'. When summer came, we all flocked to the Upper Arlington pools. We took swim lessons in the morning, and then we would return in the afternoon for the free swim. My mom was always very agreeable about us going to the pool, but she would do things like cover us in vinegar to stop sunburn. If it was very hot, she wouldn't let us go because of the fear of catching polio, a disease that I knew about, because several of my friends had it, but I was never worried because it seemed to be more like the flu. The sad thing was, and I never learned this until later, that once you got over being bedridden with the 'flu' part of polio, that many of your limbs might not work. Sad, very sad.

Well, there were several girls, all who attended Jones Junior High, who were always at the pool. They were all very well-endowed and quite playful. However, one day, one of them, who went by our name for her 'Bubbles' because of her huge tits, had her period. She would get out of the pool, head to a diving block and be dripping very dark blood down her leg. It was sickening. She was totally unaware of what was going on, mainly because most of the blood was dripping from between her legs and down the back side of her thighs and calves. We finally left, but that scene has stuck in my mind until this day. It sure didn't help her reputation, because as the word got out, the realities of the situation were grossly exaggerated.

We all wore Speedos for our first 2–3 years of going to the pool. For the guys, it really wasn't a big deal, but for the girls, it sure gave us a visual of how they were evolving in puberty.

By the third grade, many of the girls were bursting little boobs, and we loved to check out their nipples, especially when the pool was rather cold. By the fourth grade, pubic hair was popping out of many of those suits, and by fifth grade, some pretty healthy outlines of developing vaginas were present. As a highly immature social colony, we all listened to gossip, and if anything sexual was ever the flavor of the day, it got everyone's attention. About the time we were between 4th and 5th grade, word got out that many of the cheerleaders at Watterson High School were pregnant. This was fantastic news, because for many of us, we were just learning how someone might get pregnant. Now we could see it for real and conjure up some ideas of how this happened!

Watterson was a Catholic High School on the north end of Columbus, which was attended by many former St. Agatha students. One of the most iconic was named Mickey. He had supposedly gotten his cheerleader girlfriend, Susie, pregnant. Mickey was a spots superstar and more or less an icon that every guy wanted to aspire to his level of success. In those days, you got someone pregnant, you either disappeared for six months and went to Aunt Jenny's home in some remote part of the USA, or you got married. The core to the rumors about Mickey and Susie was now he would lose his scholarship to OSU. No one really knew whether he had any scholarship offers or not.

What I found to be really intriguing was that one day at the pool, while a bunch of us were walking back from the drug store with our bags of candy, we ran into Mickey and Susie, and damn was she pregnant! She had a very pronounced baby bump. I could say that I was an expert on baby bumps, because my mother had been pregnant about ten times, but our curiosity was more on just what had happened, and what did it feel like, to get this girl in situation. Hmm?

We were now becoming more sexually socialized, and that can be scary. The year before this, I was probably the most socially sensitive grade schooler than anyone alive. However, over the years, I certainly learned that there is so much that the educational system does to students to traumatize and stereotype them that is criminal.

My situation centers on the fact that by the time I was in third grade, I was not reading anywhere near most of my classmates. I was avoiding reading and starting to become increasingly distractible. Well, this naturally initiated a conference between my parents and my 3rd grade teacher, who was my cousin. There, all of a sudden, was a certain 'hush hush' atmosphere in the McNally house. First to come was while I was eating breakfast on a Saturday morning. My dad came down and told me that we had a meeting that morning. I tried to get some information on who we were going to meet, but he sure didn't give me any.

Well, we headed down to the Children's Hospital in Columbus. The place is long gone as far as I know, but I sure was curious as to why would I be going to a hospital on a Saturday, especially when I felt fine. Well, my mother finally sprung it on me that I was going to see a psychologist. Great! What the fuck was a psychologist? When I got a pretty lame explanation, we were soon there, and I was escorted to his office.

It seemed to me he was more invested in answering his phone and making phone calls; however, when time permitted, he would throw a question my way. He then tossed a problem in my lap, that I still remember that I just wasn't sure was the proper answer. He said that he was sending me to the river to get exactly 2 gallons of water. He was giving me a 3-gallon pail and a 5-gallon pail. How was I going to go about getting exactly 2 gallons of water? It was kinda like a MENSA question whereas the answer was so obvious, it was silly, but I was stumped.

Well, the good news was, I came out of the session with a FSIQ of 118, so I had the bullets to tackle any academic challenge, but I was now being referred to the Child Guidance Clinic for reading skills training. Well, what I soon learned, that added insult to injury, was a classmate, a little wallflower named Mary, headed to the same place with me, and that we were going to carpool! Whoa! This brought about some great social anxiety. She was not cool. She was still physically a little girl, plus she had red hair, which was also not cool.

If I remember correctly, her folks owned the Rolls Royce dealership in Columbus, so we got transported in the height of luxury. It was great, because the back end of that vehicle, like most cars of the 60s, was very large. So, I could sit very far from her as we traveled to downtown Columbus. The good news was, this whole experience ignited in me my goal of "I'll become the best reader in the world…if this is what I have to do to get out of this commitment."

Well, low and behold, there were several variables playing into my reading lagging ability. One was, I needed glasses! Dah! The other was, my reading counselor, a nun, no less, felt that I needed high-interest reading material. So, my folks got me the Hardy Brothers' books. They also got a set of Tom Swift books. I also started collecting coins. Mostly to do this, you need to read many publications about which coins are worth collecting. So, sci-fi, numismatics, and glasses got me rolling, and by the time I reached the 8th grade, I was one of the better readers in the whole school. My vocabulary had increased at a remarkable rate, and in the 7th grade, I was voted the most outstanding debater by the school. Reading 'I am Legend' by Richard Matheson was a hallmark in my life. I felt that I had established myself as a legend, because I was not going to let the system try and fix my shortcomings. I could do it by myself, if I could capture all of the right ingredients.

Pubescence

Whew! What a part of life to analyze and explore. In Golden Bear land, the process is rather intense. Not only are you dealing with the day-to-day complications of who has said what to whom, or who likes whom, but you also deal with the social pressure of debutants, cotillions, organized country club parties, sweet-sixteen parties and a whole bunch of other nonsense. By 6th grade, girl and boy parties were starting to get organized. The first one I was invited to was a hayride out at Darby Farms, organized by the two lesbian mothers who had divorced their husbands so that they could live together. Word had it that many of the other mothers were very cautious letting their little girls or guys go on this activity, but all caved in and let the parties begin. All of the 'cool' girls were there: Mary, Maggie, Marlania, Eileen, Claudia, Rosalie, and many others. These first few were already well-developed, emerging ladies, who had perky breasts and shapely buns; plus, they all had a certain flirtatiousness to their personalities. Well, it wasn't long before a game of 'spin the bottle' got organized on the back of the hay wagon.

At first, I wasn't even sure of what the game involved, but I quickly learned as I watched Claudia put a big lip lock on Johnny H. I was at first surprised, but it made sense that the girls had worked a safety net for themselves in the game. If they got the bottle pointing at them, they could choose whom to kiss or choose whom to slap. So now, the test would come as to who the girls thought were ugly, or not worth kissing. Sure enough, it happened. Mary, the daughter of one of the mothers who had organized this shindig, got picked, and it was her turn to kiss Harry. Well, Harry had popularity because he was an outstanding athlete, but he looked rough and rugged, so she slapped him, and I mean, she damn near decked him. Wow! What a bitch.

I was a guy with much testosterone, and I could see that Mary was a pick of the litter and well worth chasing after. Luckily, that night, I got a few kisses and no slaps. So, I made it through with my dignity intact. My plans were to slowly start to pursue Mary.

Having a gal and going steady, at any age, was a Golden Bear social expectation. It gave you status, much like a new car or new house, or joining the country club would for an adult. So, I jumped right in on trying to secure this girlfriend thing. My parents being the very formal people they were wanted me to invite Mary for Sunday dinner. This was always in our formal dining room. White shirts and ties, as well as dresses for the ladies. A rack of lamb, chateau brion, prime rib or slow roasted chickens, were usually on the menu. Every so often, we'd have rock Cornish hens stuffed with rice, or fresh walleye with hush puppies, and then there were special meals for the various holidays. Near the beginning of Lent, we'd have Jambalaya with fresh shrimp and ochre- a carryover from my mother's southern roots.

I was in the 4th grade. My girlfriend's mom, who was an artist, was getting a divorce from her father, which in itself was great gossip, but what really juiced up the situation was one of my buddies, a guy I had grown up with, had parents who were divorcing as well. To many, it seemed like an epidemic. The drama really surfaced when the two artist moms moved in together. Their relationship as lesbians really got the rumor mill spinning. In the years to come, never, ever, even once did my girlfriend mention a word about her mother's relationship with Phil's mom. Even the family denied the existence of anything going on out of the ordinary.

Mary came, after I reluctantly called her, all the while fearing rejection. She dressed up for the occasion, and we had this rather stifled dinner experience, but hey, for a couple of 12-year-olds, it wasn't bad. It at least allowed me to more or less put my tag on her so that I could say that we were going together.

Now, life was getting complicated. I had to juggle going to school, trying out and playing sports, conditioning myself, visiting Mary at home, learning how to play the guitar, doing chores at home, and reluctantly doing homework; plus, my involvement in collecting coins was intense. It brought out my best talents. I needed to research what was hot and needed to be collected. I had to plan my trips to the bank. I needed to negotiate my 'spot' money from my folks so that I could afford to purchase $100–$200 worth of change each day, spend time reviewing these coins, and then going back to exchange them for fresh change at the bank within a day or so. I also needed to maintain contacts at the banks who would give me coins that had not been surveyed. I used to ink mark my rolled coins with a special insignia, so that I never got the same coins twice.

During these times, I would also lift weights in my bedroom and crank on my guitar, to the point that the neighbors 1, 2, 3, 4 and more houses down would call to have me turn down the volume. What came last was homework, because frankly, I never saw any point in it. It was not challenging; some I didn't understand and most of it had little to no relevance to the greater world.

I knew, however, that my strengths were in the area of being creative and my strong business acumen. Several of us shared in the same skills and desires. So, one day, I instigated a physical confrontation with the black janitor at the school, named Herb. He was one tough cookie. I think that he had played football at OSU, but he had gotten his girl pregnant, gotten married, and now had to be a janitor, drive a bus, and do other miscellaneous jobs to stay afloat. Well, I got him in a bit of a tussle in the boys' bathroom and when it was done, he had me against the wall. Herb was making this guy thing ubiquitous statement, "Well, have you had enough?"

"Heck yes," was my response, because little did he know, I had lifted his master key out of his pocket. Now we were locked, cocked and ready to unlock, doc.

Well, Gary, Toots, and I were ready to go into business. The school sold lunch tokens every Monday, five for a dollar-twenty-five, which got you lunch for 5 days. Well, we were invested in the American way, so we started selling 5 lunches for a buck. We started small, so that no one would notice the shortfall in school sales. We even expanded to the younger grades. That master key let us in to the cashier's room and we would extract just enough tokens, so that we could maintain regular sales without making it too obvious that many were missing. This little scam went on for months. We were making enough cash to offset our meager allowances.

I was lucky enough to have a large bedroom that was over our garage that afforded us room for weightlifting, poker playing, guitar jamming and even sleeping, if you had time. We soon got into playing poker with our lunch token profits, and we would even discuss other scams that we could get into to increase our cash flow. The nice thing was, I was winning at poker, so my bank roll was increasing at an impressive rate.

It was quickly becoming springtime in the year 1963. We had already experienced the Tuesday in March snowstorm that closed the schools and had allowed us to head down to George Zeisler's Records and pick up the first 45 RPM record release from The Beatles. We even got many of the business card promos of the 'Beatles are coming' stickers that just showed the outline of the haircuts of the fabulous four.

There was an Easter dance scheduled at the St. Agatha gym for all of the high schoolers, mostly the guys and gals from Watterson High School and a few of the Golden Bears from Upper Arlington. It was one of those Easters, like the one in 2008, that came very early in the year. Yes, it snowed! Great, cause my buddies and I were there to work clean-up. We quickly used the master key to open the coat room and started taking coats, umbrellas and purses. Naturally, we collected tips and charged for coat room service.

What wasn't apparent to us, is how we were developing a Golden Bear perception that nothing could happen to us. We were invincible. There were no consequences for our behavior. There was this emerging character trait emerging in all of us, "It's okay to take what you want, when you want, the Golden Bear way!" Without knowing it, we were becoming CRO '67!

Well, we continued to use the key—which to this day, I still have—mostly to enter the gym on Sundays to play b-ball. It was great recreation, and in reality, schools are continuously criticized for not being open enough for public use. Well, we were trendsetters. We were using the gym a lot. We also used the Jones Junior High gym by climbing to the top of the four-story building and going through a fire escape. Arlington buddies of mine, Alf, Budda and Katman showed us the way, so we had two gyms to play b-ball. We also did gymnastics and the rope climb.

One Saturday, Gary F. and Johnny G. stopped by. Usually, we would head downtown Columbus on the 'blue' bus that mostly carried whites. The 'yellow' bus carried coloreds. A thing that wouldn't happen in modern times. Our usual agenda was to go downtown, head to Flag Brothers Shoes and purchase a new pair of 'nigger diggers'. Between Richmond Bro's and Flag's, they had a corner on the market for fighting shoes. These shoes were downright dangerous. They had toes that were so pointed, it was hard to believe that anyone could even put their foot in them, plus the price was right. The shoes were so cheaply made that buying a new pair every two weeks or so was no big deal. Then we'd head down to the Ohio Palace or one of the other classic theaters. We'd pay for the children's matinee, and once it was over, we'd head to the top of the second balcony and hide between the seats until the main show started. These were usually double features, so we would get a lot of entertainment for 50 cents. Once out of the theater, we'd go to White Castle, get 5 burgers each, fries, and a large pop. Usually, this was about $1.95 each.

On this Saturday, Johnny G. had us getting off the bus in Grandview, a more traditional, lower-class suburb of Columbus, and we were headed to the home of a chick whom he had met. We entered the home, and it's just this cute little pubescent girl and her brother. Her parents are gone. So, we sit down on the couch in the basement and start watching Lex Mayer sponsored wrestling. Soon, Johnny is massaging her tits on the outside of her shirt, and she leans over and starts kissing me and stroking my cock. Gary was in the back room shooting pool. Johnny's hand went up one side of her shirt and mine the other. We each had a handful of very perky tits, still in the bra, and she was really working my cock from the outside of my pants and kissing me with her tongue down my throat. Well, as one might guess, noises were heard upstairs, and her parents came home. We scattered like Marines running from a Claymore mine. We went and hid in the furnace room. Her father discovered us in no time and escorted us to the door. No one said much. We quickly departed the neighborhood and headed to the bus stop to finish our journey downtown. This was a move in the right direction. I was now trying to figure out just what one needed to do when he had a hot chick! This girl was light years past me!

I remember, though, that spring, when there were flash floods, reading about her younger brother being washed down a storm drain and never being recovered. That left a very hollow feeling in me, and what's even sadder is that I can't remember her name as of today.

Well, just before school was out for that summer, there was a big dance planned up at Upper Arlington, the home of the Golden Bears. We all planned to go, and it was a good chance to meet new girls and to also hopefully hook up with one of our clique gals. I never was much of a dancer, but at this event, there were clack-stick contests, hula-hoop events and a bunch of other fun stuff. I think that the inventor of WHAM-O was behind all of these products. We were all having a lot of fun. There had been only one major fight that I knew of, which involved two of the Titans. Tom K., a Golden Bear, and Frank S. from Watterson. Frank had blasted Tom K. right on the top of his nose, so he was bleeding like a stuck pig. Otherwise, all was peaceful, until Rick G., son of my absolute favorite baseball coach started confronting me, so I went after him.

Well, when that fracas was over, his supposed $100.00 shirt was all ripped to hell, and I had him in a chokehold that made him say, "Uncle." We never had any more encounters, and I never held any ill-will toward him. Mostly because his father, a former pitching coach for the Pittsburgh Pirates, was like a surrogate father to me. In the next few years, he lifted my ego and skills about tenfold. He instilled confidence in me that made me feel like I could succeed at anything, and he was never critical of my mistakes. So, I'm not even sure what ignited the conflict between me and his son. I would guess that it was my volatility and lack of self-confidence. I would overreact in situations and try to control what I couldn't control with my very efficient fighting skills and strength. There too, had to be a quasi-sibling rivalry here. Ric was an only child. Surely, I was jealous!

Well as this dance was winding down, Gary F., my buddy, and Toots got together, and Gary shared with us that 'Bubbles' wanted a ride home. Toots and I were both kinda like, "No way! How will you ever get rid of her?" But Gary was insistent. Toots had a brand-new 406 Ford Galaxy that he purchased for cash from his many entrepreneurial ways. Interestingly, he didn't even have a license yet, but again, in the heyday of the Golden Bears, who cares? Anyway, Toots had a disabled mother, whom he needed to drive to church, to the store and other places, so his parents were very generous as far as giving permission.

Well, Gary, Bubbles and I got into the back of the 406, while Toots took over the front. Off we went, and sure enough, Gary was making out with her, and she had her right hand on my cock. Whew, that felt good. She then changed positions and started making out with me and before you knew it, she was stroking each of our cocks and Toots had parked the car and he was fingering her vagina from the front seat. Well, she definitely introduced something new when she slid down and started to suck on my very erect cock. Damn, what a rush. Gary was busy trying to get her blouse off, and once she did, it unleashed a wonderful set of tits. Well, that foursome continued for another hour or so. I just remember that cumming in her mouth was a wonderful experience, and sucking on her tits was just as glorious.

We dropped her off at her house, and it was as if nothing had ever happened. She tended to hang with a pretty rough crowd of outsiders, but never were there any repercussions from this encounter. It was as though it never happened, and she was just as happy as we were that it happened. Overall, it was a great introduction to a shared sexual experience. It far transcended just playing with yourself. What was most intriguing was, just how did Bubbles know all of that technique?

Well, this and those very few experiences prior to this unleashed the tiger inside me, and any other teen, as to what is in store for you as an aspiring Golden Bear. Little did we know at the time how disillusioned we all were. What waited for us in the real world, in the years yet to come, was going to be a rude awakening.

St. Agatha was well along in the building of a new church, which was a perfect location to set up liaisons with my girlfriend, Mary. Our first encounters, in the late spring, were in the baseball dugouts at Northern Park, next to St. Agatha. We would sit in the dugouts, exchanging a bunch of worthless chat and then finally start kissing. The best I ever got from her in that situation was some bare tit. This was nice, but the pizzazz of grabbing flesh and having someone stroking on your cock just wasn't there. So, we progressed to the construction zone of the new church. It produced some new encounters, but this pretty much stayed the same. I got to massage her pussy from the outside of her panties, and more playfully tease her tits, but it was the same old, same old. So, we never got to the point of where we shouldn't have been, however it was worth a try.

Partying, playing cards and trying to hook up with the gals became our social priorities. It was the Golden Bear way to go for the gusto. Now for me, getting noticed revolved mostly around my speed, strength and as the girls would tell me, my cute looks. I was also developing my guitar playing skills, so the future looked bright as far as getting into a band.

When we finally made it to the 9th grade, our social lives were starting to sizzle, and the thought of becoming a Golden Bear the following year was very exciting. I had made a lot of connections with students from Jones Junior High over the summer, and they were all destined for Upper Arlington High School. They were a wild bunch, and they readily accepted me and my friends because we could only further their pursuit of cheap thrills.

Making money continued to be a high priority, and being a caddy at Scioto Country Club was a good way to go. However, the competition was fierce. Many of us would ride our bikes to school, and once that last bell rang, off we went to try and catch a single or a double at the club. It was always a mad dash.

Many of my classmates would get pretty malicious and do things like slash your bike tires or wire your front tire to the bike rack with a coat hanger. No one locked their bike in those days, because it was pretty rare that anyone would steal your bike. Phil, whose mother was one of the lesbian moms, was notorious for screwing with your bike so that he could be the first to the caddy shack. It finally boiled down to a few of us having to rough him up to get that stopped. Tom D., a very strong, significantly deaf buddy of mine, took care of bouncing Phil around. So, for the rest of the fall, we didn't have any more problems.

Tom D. was in class by himself, literally. He was strikingly handsome and very funny. He was also quite sexually precocious. He was known for getting into trouble, and he enjoyed it. Lucky for him, there were no small buses taking kids to school. A product named Flubber was very popular in those days. It was rubbery substances that became popular after the Disney movie of the same name. Well, the stuff bounced like a golf ball on steroids. It was sold at the GC Murphy store at Lane Shopping Center, and Tom would go there daily and shoplift a package of the stuff. Soon, he had accumulated a huge ball of this goop. He would roll it up into tiny little balls, and when Sister Shaun Marie would be working at the board, Tom would throw a handful of these mini balls toward her.

Well, the stuff bounced so fast, it was hard to even see it. Sister would turn around and look as if she had seen a ghost, everyone would then look busy, and then she would go back to whatever she was writing on the board. One day, Tom really got wild. While Sister was working at the board, he let go with this Flubber ball that bounced off the board, hit the floor, then bounced to the ceiling, hitting the black-light globe and breaking it. Shaun Marie turned around and literally ran at Tom D. He took one glance at the fire in her eyes, smiled, then turned to the windows behind him, jumped up on the heat register, opened the window, and jumped! It had to be one of the funniest things I had ever seen in my life. She started yelling at him, two-stories down below, but he was off running. She continued to yell, "I'm going to get Father Kennedy to take care of you!" Then someone chimed in, "He can't hear you, Sister!" Tom rarely wore his hearing aids, so 'huh' was his most common comment.

The rest of that day, we all kept eyes on our work, and no one dared to act out. We could see that Sister, who was in her first year as a teaching nun, was on the verge of going over the edge. Eventually, I think that we pushed her there. She was a cute, young lady, petite body, fair skin and she looked 'fuckable'. It made no sense that she was a nun.

It doesn't snow much in Columbus, but it does get very cold. When November came, we started to get one or two inches of snow a week. Some of our older buddies showed us the fine art of 'scitching'. This is where you sneak up on a stopped car or truck, take a good hold of the bumper, and when the vehicle takes off, so do you, but you need a nice coating of ice or snow on the road to make this work, as well as leather soles on your shoes!

Well, as winter marched on, we started to become real experts at hooking up free rides when the conditions were right. We would travel all over town, holding on to the bumpers of numerous cars. Sometimes, the ice spray got to be a bit too much, and our gloves would get soaked. So, we would stop by a church and search through the lost and found, or we would head to Lane Avenue Shopping Center, go to the Union Store, pick out some nice new leather gloves, and put them on my charge account. That, in itself, was so indicative of the Golden Bears lifestyle. If you need it, buy it, charge it, but get it! There's no delay of gratification. It was a society that did not know self-denial. The typical Golden Bear only knew self-indulgence. Our 'ID' influence was sure repressing the influence of our superegos.

It was fast approaching, the holiday season of our 8th grade year, and alcohol was making its way into our social lives. When my parents traveled, I would host poker games, and in would come the Stroh's beer. We even started to smoke, and the butts of choice were Lucky Strikes, Winstons, Pall Malls and Camels. Hit Parade and Chesterfields were popular when they were mailing out free samples. So, a few of my neighborhood buddies and I, including Sue D., would raid mailboxes and take all the sample cigarettes. Then we would sit in the woods behind Sue's house and smoke until we were about to pass out. Sue was a year older, an Upper Arlington ninth grader and very well-endowed.

I always had fantasies of sexually messing around with her, but she just never gave out the signals that would invite a pass. However, years later, she ended up living with my best friend, who was fucking her and a few friends of hers on a regular basis. I seriously begrudged my reluctance of not jumping her bones back then, but hey, what did I know? Nothing! Interestingly, when it came to smoking and the decision to smoke, I still, to this day, have a Popular

Mechanics Magazine from the era and on the back cover, there is an ad that reads, "9 out of 10 doctors who smoke, smoke Camels!" I would imagine that those 9 doctors are very dead by now!

That just goes to show you how society, in Golden Bear land, and the rest of the U.S.A., was caught in a vacuum of denial. It was as though our generation, and the numerous resources and opportunities afforded to the Golden Bears, allowed us to be some of the first to push the envelope of life and rules, morals and traditions. We, in essence, were the pioneers boldly exploring behaviors and experiences that started the process of shattering the Pleasantville façade of the times. Unknown to us, we were seeding a sub-cultured revolution, hence CRO '67!

Gangs

Now, most people do not associate gang activity with the rich and famous, but guess what—by definition alone, Upper Arlington is as much a ghetto as is the Watts section of L.A. Gangs do very much exist in the land of white picket fences and black-faced lantern men, who decorated far too may driveways and the entrance to Scioto Country Club.

The 'Bombas', organized by a Jones Junior High flunky named Morales, was my first association with a group that wanted to cause chaos wherever they went. A lot of the 'Bomba' stuff was harmless, and the name came off of the movie series of African Adventures that were aired every Saturday. Somehow, we all got on the same bowling team, and together, the 'Bombas' would bowl on Saturdays. We started planning a New Year's Eve party at Morales' house about Thanksgiving time. He had the perfect place. He lived in a three-story house in old Arlington with his mother. He had the entire third floor to himself. He had a living room, bedroom and bathroom, plus a screened-in porch that overlooked the backyard. He even had his own private outside staircases, so that we could come and go as we pleased. He even had a kitchen with a fridge!

To plan for the perfect party, we needed to start stock-piling our liquor supply. So, each of us: Pat, Gary, Tom D., Morales, Rick, Gary K., Jimmy H., Rick B., Rick Mac., Toots, Billy C., Rick W., and several others started slowly draining booze from our parents' liquor cabinets and bars. Soon, we all had gallons of pure zombies. You name it, we had it, and it was all mixed together. Plus, we did some 'garaging' and collected quite a few six packs of Stroh's, PBR and Schlitz. When New Year's arrived, we all started to flow in Morales' dormitory domain. We had sacks, bags, and boxes of much hooch. Our beer was mostly warm, but the drinking and partying started quickly. Bo Didley music was a passion of Morales, and since many of us were aspiring guitar players, we didn't protest. Bo played loud throughout the night, but what soon happened was a wake-up call to us all, but none of us ever really heeded this experience over the long-haul. Our buddy, Pat, called 'PT' was guzzling Peter Pan jars full of Zombie Mix.

PT started getting sick, and he literally passed out and hit the floor. To contain his puking, he was placed in the bathtub, where he continued to puke. He then turned blue and started shaking. We were all too drunk to do anything other than wonder just how sick he was. The notion of alcohol poisoning was not something that we were aware of, and based upon what most of us now know, who are still alive, he could have died that night. Luckily, PT survived the incident, but it took the better part of the rest of our school break for him to get right. He was just one of the many of us who had alcoholic parents, siblings, and close friends who just wandered through life. Unfortunately, this was just the beginning of him entering into a slice of the Golden Bear culture that transcended fun. We were now all starting to walk a tight rope in life that could, and would, have serious and tragic consequences. Death was now becoming an ever-present consequence of poor choices. The Bombas was just a training exercise before we would join CRO '67.

Entering the Work World

By the 1st of the New Year, I was offered a Citizen Journal newspaper route. I had previously subbed for guys on vacations during the summer, and now I had the opportunity to have my own route. I agreed, because I figured that I could earn about $11–$12 per week. I had about 52 customers, and the great news was, the Citizen Journal did not have a Sunday edition! I really liked the fact that this was a morning route, because I'm very much a morning person.

The one bummer, as I soon learned, was that the guy I got the route from had already collected all the Christmas tips. So, I was starting off fresh, and that I would have to borrow money from my parents to pay for my first week of papers. The route was down in old Arlington, south of Lane Avenue, in a great neighborhood. Plus, I got to ride by Bev DeAngelo's house each morning, who was going with my buddy and neighbor. I just wanted to catch a flash of her, which of course never happened. In those days, she was just like the rest of us, cute as a 'bug's ear' and petite. Her brother was a musician, so I was interested in maintaining good ties with him and her. Her dad was a manager of one of the TV stations, and I'm sure that somehow figured into her great rise to stardom. She was one talented little lady.

The Citizen Journal was dropped off at my house at about 5:00 a.m. One day a week, there was a tabloid that came with the paper also. It was only for customers who subscribed to it. I would always check it out, because it had a lot of racy photos and stories. Much cleavage and juicy stories highlighted this example of yellow journalism. So, each day, I would roll, and sometimes stuff newspapers and load them into my canvas newspaper bag. All the while, I'd be sipping hot chocolate. I was ready to go by 5:45 a.m. So, I would hop on my bike and head south on Andover, hoping that the roads weren't too slippery. There were many days I would hit the asphalt like a falling sack of potatoes. I would usually smoke as I delivered the papers, and my baseball skills helped me a lot. I would ride right through everyone's front lawn and toss the papers on their front porch.

I had a few customers, like Woody Hayes, who had special delivery requests. Woody liked his paper put inside his front screen door, so I would always oblige, because I didn't want that tub of lard, short-tempered football coach coming after me. It paid off, mostly because he was rarely home. He was off, staying in the sports dormitory at OSU, so I would deal with his wife, Anne. She was a charming little lady, and she would always tip me 50 cents per week. That was a lot in that time, and I really appreciated it. I had another customer, Bonnie C's family, and the rumor was her dad was mafia; whether he was or not, he sure looked the part. He was a tall, dark Italian. He always wore classy, pin-striped wool suits with cuff links, a stud in his tie, and he would never say much. Frankly, he scared the shit out of me, and if you know Columbus, there is a huge population of Italians. Most resided in Grandview, but he lived in the more elite section of Upper Arlington. I would always park my bike, walk to the front of the house and place the paper in the holder below the mailbox. My Italian friends always reinforced to me that this was a good decision. It showed respect.

Saturdays were always special on the newspaper delivery route. My buddies Phil, Marty, Toots, and I all delivered within the same area, so when we were done, we would head to Lane Shopping Center and help ourselves to a box or two of freshly delivered donuts that were sitting outside one of the pharmacies. Then we would head to Toots' house, because he had an apartment-like setup in his garage, and we could go up there, stay warm, eat donuts, and sip hot chocolate. It was heaven! His parents would never say a word, because Toots never did anything wrong. To them, he was a perfect child, which is partially why he had a brand-new 406 Galaxy in his garage, no license, and always a big smile on his face. Collecting was also an activity that we tried to coordinate among ourselves. We would do this at night, and we would eventually end up at McKinley's Pharmacy, which had a soda fountain in the back, and we would eat burgers, fries and the best hot fudge sundaes this side of the Mississippi! Sometimes though, our Golden Bear adolescent arrogance would get the best of us.

The streets of old Arlington were lined with tall gas streetlights. Well, we would often regress to using these for target practice. Usually, we would use slingshots with BB's, but with the better Wham-O slingshots, we'd use marbles. Dang! They could blow out a light with one shot. One night, Toots and I were outside Schmidt's house, and if you know Columbus, this is a family with a multi-generational investment in the German restaurant business. Well, we ran into one stubborn light. I had shot at it several times with marbles, and the frosted glass had broken, but the gas continued to burn. Finally, as it became time to run before someone decided to call the police, Toots grabs a large chuck of concrete, obviously broken off from the curb, and he chucks it at the top of the light. *Wham*! There was an explosion and then a fire! It was time to boogie and get the hell out of there! After that, we moved our target practice to the Scioto River.

Soon, I was getting a visit from my paper route manager, who informed me that he was getting indirect reports of vandalism, yard damage and other complaints from the area of my route. I listened but never admitted nor denied anything. I figured that he would go grill the others, who he knew were my chums, about any transgressions. One snowy, miserable day, he stopped by and had some sort of complaint that he was lodging against me, and it was time for me to stand my ground. However, there was the reality that I was getting the papers to everyone on time. The papers were delivered, folded and dry, and collections were up to date, but now, I was making the transition from boy to cocky teenager, which preceded being a young, dumb adult.

Well, I think the district paper dude was Pascal, who tossed the bundle of papers out to me and basically threatened me that I was on my last leg as a delivery boy. So, I picked up the large bundle of papers and I tossed them on the hood of his car. "If you think that you can do it better, go for it!" was my response. Well, he softened immediately. He didn't want to deal with being chased by dogs, go door-to-door 50-some-odd times, put papers in doorways and try and figure out how to collect, so now he was kissing my ass. Great! My days of being slave labor were going to quickly come to an end. Spring was here, it was time to try out for baseball, and soon, we'd be at the pool. So, being a paperboy was going to quickly come to an end. My involvement with the band was increasing also, so soon, a cashflow from that was imminent.

I figured that spring break from school was the perfect time to sever my ties with the paper. I typed up and delivered a real nice 'it's been real' note that I included in all of my papers, to forewarn my customers that I would be moving on. This produced a huge number of tips. I think that I collected twice in one week just to fill my bank account. It worked, and I got huge handshakes, offers for other jobs, kisses on the forehead, and much more. Then I kissed Pascal goodbye. Unfortunately, shortly thereafter, he was killed in a one-car crash. He lived near the Scioto River, and he came down his street, headed toward Route 33, but failed to stop at his intersection. His car literally became airborne, taking off the tops of the trees next to the river, and he crashed down below. Reportedly, he was dead on impact. Very hard to believe, but a reality we all had to deal with. All of us in the Golden Bear vacuum just took this in stride. No emotion, no reaction, no response to his young family. To us, our lives went on. Completely cold!

Spring weather arrived, and now it was time for baseball. I was most interested in playing for the Upper Arlington leagues, and I wanted Don G. as my coach. He had worked with me before, and my respect for him was huge. He believed in me, and that really helped to lift my self-confidence. Overall, I had a fantastic season, usually playing third base and lead-off in the batter line up. My speed was what impressed coach the most, as well as my aggressive style. I never hesitated to knock a baseman out of position. I remember once putting a third baseman, David, into the stands, when he tried to tag me out on a steal. What became my Achilles heel was when my parents would show up for a game. This was not something that they would usually do, but when they did, I would fall apart. I was so bad in one game, with numerous errors and poor batting, as well as no stealing of bases, that Coach G. pulled me from the game. This was psychologically devastating to me, because I heard comments from other players on the team like "Well, now others of us can have a chance at being all-stars…" That hurt. I resigned myself to the fact that my future lay in other sporting events, maybe fighting as an amateur at the Columbus Athletic Club.

Before we knew it, it was summer, and many major transitions were in the future for all of us. For work, I got hooked up with a door-to-door magazine selling gig. I was playing in a band, and I now was connected with the Columbus Athletic Club, training with Fraiser Ferguson to become an athlete of status. The magazine selling was quite an adventure, because it dealt with linking up with some pretty seedy characters. We headed to these small Ohio towns to sell costly subscriptions to mostly a bunch of dumb, uninformed, white trash. One thing that did happen in this experience was that I gained a much greater appreciation for people to get educated. Damn, there is a lot of dumb out there! This was before major credit cards. People would still jump on the chance to purchase something that they probably didn't need, or could do without, but since there was no money changing hands, they would go for it. This helped me, but I always had a sick feeling about people who would eventually get billed for hundreds of dollars of mostly worthless magazines. I bet many couldn't even read. It was almost a culture of the white trash to have magazines lying around as a form of status.

On the weekends, I would head to the Athletic Club and train. They had an elevated track that I would run along with strong man Ferguson, but I couldn't make the distance because I was so fast that I would run into the wall within the first quarter of the track. Marty, Phil, Tom, Toots, and I would then be pointed to the weight room and the pool. The latter was unreal, because in these days, the guys would swim naked! This was not something we were used to. Man, did I see some ugly bodies! Yuk! But the training was invaluable, because my speed, strength, and my athletic abilities were increasing. I remember one evening, when I was walking home from the Arlington Recreation Center (ARC), I ran into Mike C. This was Marty's older brother who thought he was some sort of tough guy. I didn't want any trouble, so I took off running, like a scared deer, headed toward my house. My parents were gone, and my grandmother was home to watch over us.

Well, I made it to my garage, but sure enough, the side door was locked. Mike was on my ass in a heartbeat. Then, it became evident that the days of this older punk hassling me were over. I came down on him like stink on shit. I picked him up over my head and crashed his lame head in the concrete floor of our garage. I then proceeded to beat the living shit out of this maggot. My grandmother opened the door after hearing the ruckus and chastised me for being the ruffian. I promise you, that Mike C. never even looked cross-eyed at me every again. One down, many more to go! I gained one insight, that when I got riled up, my strength almost tripled. I bounced him around like a rubber ball, and I thoroughly enjoyed every moment of it. However, as a reputation grows, so do the challenges.

As we started to evolve as teens, it was clear that you were defined as a person by what you looked like, what you could do and who you hung out with. Your status was also elevated if you had a reputation that preceded you. Like, if you were a guy and tough, especially if you had beaten the ass of another guy who also had a reputation, then you were almost talked about as a living legend. The same dynamic still exists in the ghetto to this day. Older brothers started to emerge as legends. Just knowing the names of certain toughs carried street credit. As we neared the time to pick and choose a high school, names of the very tough started to be names that were remembered. Mickey MalCurry, Frank Strange, Brian Nielson, Sean Kelleher, Mike Hillard, Tony Scartz and others were the folk heroes of fighting throughout our end of town. Many of these guys were headed to the Catholic schools, and their reputations spoke volumes about how tough they were.

Now I was in a transition dilemma. Aquinas High School, an all-boys institution, run by priests who reportedly would kick your ass just for fun, was the alma mater of my father and all of his brothers. They talked about me going there. I wasn't keen on the idea, because not only were there not any girls, but the school was right in the middle of the black ghetto. This ghetto was like a 'mini Watts'. Aquinas High School was to be closing, and the students who were already enrolled could finish out their high school years there, but no new classes were going to be enrolled. That was a relief. So now, the decision was made immediately. We just let the calendar days slip by, and soon, we were in the summer before high school. My sights were set on Upper Arlington, but my parents thought otherwise.

Summer of 1963

Well, our activities started to become day to day, and we mostly just hung around the basketball court at Marty's house, and waited to see what the night might bring. My girlfriend, Mary, moved with her mother and younger sister to Phoenix, Arizona, so hooking up with a new chick was a priority. I was going to Miss Mary, but life would go on. Our band was starting to pull together as a quality talent, so we were able to start booking a few gigs. Whetstone Recreation Center, on the north end of Columbus, had teen dances on a pretty regular basis. We started playing there, and lo and behold, groupies actually started to surface. One I connected with was a cute little brunette named Debbie.

She was destined to attend North High School in the fall, but that didn't faze me. North was a city school, full of a lot of low-class white folks and many who thought they were tough. I started hitchhiking to Debbie's house on a regular basis, and it became a new place to hang out. Lord, she had two older sisters. Connie, Cindy and there were about 4 younger brats. Her mom was cute and nice, and her dad was a north end tough, who was usually drunk. At times, he would try and provoke trouble, like one night, he had a straight razor and he wanted to go out on the front porch so he could show me how you fight with a razor. I went, but damn, I thought that he was going to try and kill me. I did my best to avoid his slashing at me, but luckily, his wife called him back into the house.

Whew! Like every other musically inclined teen, I was growing my hair out in the fashion of The Beatles or Stones. My hair was thick and curly and grew quickly. The girls tended to like it, but it was a red flag to many guys. You had to quickly ignore who called you a ferry, or on the way home late at night, it wasn't uncommon to get hit with eggs, rocks, stones or trash. There were times, if the conditions were right, to stand your ground and go after whatever punk was giving you shit.

A bunch of us headed off to equestrian camp that summer. Three weeks away from home at a coed camp sounded exciting. Unfortunately, we rarely got to see the girls. So, the whole experience turned into a 'sports' experience. One of the sports was conditioning for boxing, and then subsequently, if you survived the elimination rounds, you fought for a championship in your weight class. Well, I had no problem working my way through the other 142 lb. bunch, but there was one guy, who had held the welterweight title for 2 years running and was a golden gloves boxer out of Cincinnati. Him, I was cautious of.

Toward the end of our three-week stay came 'Fight Night'. It was a grand affair, because boxers of all weight classes were the entertainment of the night. There was a barbeque, pop, chips, bonfires, and a gathering of all the campers, including the girls. Now, the butterflies were beginning to collect in my stomach. I did not want to get embarrassed in front of any of these girls, and I had to fight the toughest guy in the camp. All I could fall back on was my training with Fraizer Ferguson, my weightlifting, and my speed. Somehow, though, I was hooked up with a cornerman with an Irish name like McCarthy. He talked to me as if he knew me my whole life. He gave me some pointers, and he stressed the notion of being patient and not 'jumping in' to throw a punch. Sounded like good advice!

Well, after some dazzling performances by many of the lighter fighters, it was our turn. Mike, whom I was boxing, was older than me, so he was introduced first. Then, it came time for my name to be announced, and I felt well received by the other campers, but I felt that there was a coalition of staff who wanted me to get my ass pounded. They didn't like the fact that a bunch of us had come to camp as a 'gang' of spoiled brats. Well, as Gordon Lightfoot sang, "Where does the love of God go when the waves to the minutes to hours…" It was as if time stood still, and as McCarthy gave me my last few pointers, it was time to touch gloves and let the bell ring.

Mike and I quickly squared off in the middle of the ring, and he threw an overhand right that just about put me in La La Land. I was glad to still be standing, but as he punched, and it was mostly with his right, I would counter with my left. Fortunately for me, I've always been ambidextrous, so even though I fought like a right-hander, my left was equally as powerful. When the bell rang to end round one, I could only see the inside of the ring. My mind would not let me see beyond that. McCarthy said, "You've got him worried, and he's starting to back up. Keep the pressure on him, and as soon as he drops his right hand, clock him with your right." Sounded good, but I felt like saying that I thought that I may be in real trouble out there.

Round two started with another touch of the gloves and the same circling to our lefts, Mike punching for a knockout and me countering with every blow. Then, after a solid connection with my left, he moved back just a half step, and his right hand dropped just a bit. I let go with a punch that I thought would knock his head off, and down he went! He got up before being counted out, and he finished the round. The third and final round was all mine. I went at him with both hands, and I didn't let up. He backed up the entire round, and I landed most of my punches. Both of his hands dropped, and now it was just target practice. He was finished! When the vote was tallied, I had scored a unanimous decision over the reigning champ. What really was a great culmination of the entire camp experience was that at the very last night of our stay, there was a big get-together, with a bonfire, hot dogs, and awards. I got the outstanding boxer award and outstanding athlete award. I was very proud of myself, but inside, I still struggled with self-doubt.

None of these 15 minutes of fame, plus an inflation in my reputation, would wash away the nagging fears that lurked in me and possibly most other Golden Bears. Just prior to the end of our football season in the previous fall, one early evening, when a bunch of us were playing mud ball at the local park, our coach stopped by. As he got out of his convertible Ford, big Mike, the stuttering meat head, told us we may not have practice the rest of the week. We all looked rather stunned, and then he followed it up with "We're going to war!" Man, I thought that I'd shit my pants. This was the time of the Bay of Pigs Invasion, and the whole country was put on a 'watch and wait' status.

Luckily, as the hours, days, and weeks went by, it seemed that the revolution and potential threat of Cuba attacking us started to slowly vanish, but deep inside all of our souls, lingered the notion that sooner or later, our heyday would be over, and we would be headed, as soldiers, to some conflict, somewhere. The political unrest in the world was immense.

Eagles and Yeagermeister Times

My older brother had entered a Pontifical seminary in the previous year, so he now was gone from home. It used to be a tradition in the Irish Catholic families that the oldest son entered the priesthood, so off he went. Visiting him was like taking friend chicken to an inmate at Folsom Prison. There were only about four visits per year, and they had to be outside of the seminary complex, so it usually turned out to be a cold, windy picnic in the parking lot, with a sibling who wore nothing but black.

My education was going to follow the Catholic route as well. My parents had decided, much to my chagrin, that I would become a Watterson Eagle. This would mean, the necessity to carpool and join up in an educational experience with students from all over Columbus. It was, by far, not my choice. I just wanted to follow the rest of the Golden Bears to Upper Arlington and stay within my neighborhood. Well, that wasn't going to happen.

The initial orientation to Watterson was like critical mass of the many reputations that were all coming together at once. This was not a good thing, because it only meant that you were going to confront trouble sooner or later. The good news was that I had connected well with a bunch of the St. Andrew's boys from North Arlington during the late summer, prior to the start of football practice and school. Word got out via other friends, at dances and the like, that I liked to shoot BB guns and that I hung around the river a lot, looking for critters. Well, some of the big and tough from St. Andrews liked the same kind of activities, so we eventually ended up going on excursions to the Scioto River downstream from Griggs Dam. We'd always head over to the Marble Cliff Quarry, which was heavily guarded, to swim in the limestone water pits, shoot fish and turtles, and just wander around in the huge expanse of limestone cliffs and gullies.

I met a lot of new friends, through the BB gun-filled trips, dances, band gigs, and initially at freshman football practice. The latter started off well when we were running dashes and sprints. Jesse was a senior and a bit of a football star, so he wanted to see what kinda speed the up-and-coming frosh had. Well, luckily for me, I beat him in the 100-yard dash. The coach was overheard by some other players as saying, "There's no way we're cutting him, with speed like that," but that commitment soon faded as the coach realized that I had a major attitude problem. Shoot, before I even got started in school, I was put on behavior probation, and several phone calls were made to my dad to inform him that I was being challenging of authority and non-conforming! Bullshit!

Well, football became history to me quickly, and subsequently, I wanted to wrestle, anyway. Two of my St. Agatha classmates, who had some issue with me being tougher than them, decided to go out and recruit some lard ass to try and hassle me each day. So, as the school year started, this flat-top, muffin-belly creep would purposely get in my way and do minor things to try and provoke me. However, he gave himself away when he made a statement, "You think that you're so tough." I thought that someone had given him that information. He was not bright enough to have learned that on his own.

Well, what he didn't know was that I was already hanging on by a very thin thread. One more discipline problem, and I would be beat with a belt and grounded until I was 21 years old! I figured that if I was patient enough, I would just wait the bastard out. He'd show up in the bathroom sometimes, and then I'd kick his ass from Franklin County to another county. That didn't happen, and I never saw him out on the street. Although one day, I did grab a hold of his neck and slam his fat ass against the lockers, just so he would realize who he was dealing with. He never went out for wrestling. I figured that would be a great place to crush his butterball attitude. So, I guess that I'm still waiting for that day to come.

Life really started to blossom when I was at Watterson. I could never shake the Golden Bear image with many of my classmates, because they would always hassle me over my clothes, shoes and hairstyle. Keeping my hair somewhat long was difficult. I used hairspray during the day to slick it down, and at night, I would tape it down and hairspray the hell out of it. Taking the curl out helped a lot, because it wouldn't stand up so far from my head.

Our band was starting to really rock, and we had bookings for most weekends. I was meeting friends who liked to party, so my social life was taking on a life by itself. One buddy I met at school, named John, had the ideal living situation. He lived way out on Route 33 in a large home with his parents.

His grandparents lived next door, and they had a lot of property. To a degree, it was like describing the belongings of the Beverly Hillbillies, but these were classy people. They had swimming pools, a screen picnic house, a bunk house, complete with wood burner, fancy cars, like thunderbirds, Chevy Impala convertibles, Cadillacs and other assorted classy automobiles. The grandparents were never seen, and neither was the father. The mom would show up once in a while, but usually, it was just me, my buddies, and John. Once in a while, his older brother would show up, but he stayed to himself.

Their home was always well-stocked with lots of food. Good stuff like steaks. Their bar was filled with the best liquor, and they had a gun cabinet that was filled with rifles, shotguns, pistols, and large amounts of ammunition. We started to make this place our weekly gathering spot. It was always mostly guys, but who cared; we had a good time, anyway. John's older brother soon became useful because he would buy beer for us. Now in Ohio in these days, 3.2% beer could be purchased by 18-year-olds, but in reality, any 16-year-old could pretty much go anywhere and buy anything.

We'd stay out at the bunkhouse and engage in drinking games. Usually rock, paper, match and scissors were the games to play. We would be chugging Colt 45, and I always had some tough drinking buddies to beat. Guys who later were recruited to play at Ohio State, so they had size. I had moxie and staying power, so it would take a while before any, or all of us, got sick.

Late one Friday night, after we'd been drinking pretty heavily, a car full of girls pulled up to the bunkhouse. They were just as smashed as we were. It was a very cold night, and we had the pot belly stove stoked up so hot that it glowed a dull red. Well, the girls started filing into the cabin, and I think that it was about the third girl in stumbled. She fell straight forward, and she put her hands up to break her fall. What happened left us all just staring in amazement. She fell directly into the wood burner. Her hands hit first, then the side of her face. Her flesh melted immediately, and the smell was enough to make anyone barf. Pulling her off that stove was no easy task, and this gal needed a hospital, like now!

Some of the other girls ran down to the main house to call an ambulance. The rest of us stayed with her to hold her down as she squirmed in unbelievable pain. We had to hold her by her wrists, because the palms of her hands were melted to the bone. The side of her face was about the same, with one eye burned closed, and the tip of her nose was missing. I had never seen anything, real or in fiction, like this, and neither had anyone else. The girl finally passed out, and so, Brian, Mike, and I headed for the woods to hide when the ambulance came. I think three other girls remained with their hurt buddy. She was taken to the hospital, and we never heard another word about her, nor ever knew what school she was from. To this day, I have always wondered how she recovered from that tragic accident, but again, here was an example of how our wild and reckless lifestyles had serious consequences that we were just not willing to acknowledge or grow from. The parties continued, and her accident eventually just blended into other urban legends.

Life continued to follow a pretty predictable routine for the months to come. However, I did try and split my time between my Golden Bear friends and my chums from Watterson. It was difficult, though, because there were some strong rivalries between the two schools. Football was probably the most intense. Behind the scenes was the gang activity, and in Golden Bear land, it boiled down to the CROs and ORCs. It would always boil down to who was the toughest, and the Watterson boys would usually win out. However, now, an encroachment of outlying districts was forming against UAHS.

It was a while before I learned what CRO and ORC stood for. Well, CRO was 'Cocks Reach Out' and ORC was 'Open and Ready for Cocks'. Who knows how this ever evolved, but it was a strong force within the school system. Guys and gals were recruited to join during their junior year, and then, they would run the show as seniors. The groups had sweatshirts and T-shirts with the CRO logo on them. The icon looked kinda like Heckel or Jeckel with a beer and a cigarette.

Guys usually wore black with gold insignias and the girls wore black with gold insignias. The Eagles social badges were letter jackets. There were even letter sweaters, but a guy would usually only buy one of those if he were going to give it to his girlfriend. The girls could always buy one for themselves. However, girl sports just weren't that popular in the late 60s. The good news was that I didn't have to confront this sort of social pressure yet. I had enough to manage in the present. My dad insisted that I get a letter jacket as a freshman for wrestling. I stalled. I wanted more.

My freshman year was a disaster, academically speaking. I had no interest in being successful at Watterson, and I wasn't happy in the least with my schedule. As results or pre-enrollment testing, students were placed based upon ability. So here I was, stuck in a totally college prep curriculum, when I wasn't even certain if I wanted to go to college. A career as a musician seemed much more appealing, plus I was hugely involved in coin collecting. I was taking Latin in my first year, and the only thing I learned in that entire class was how to deal with nationwide fear, confusion, and sadness.

It was just after lunch, and we were all headed to class. I entered Latin class with one of my favorite nuns, a Dominican, who was young and at times fun. It was about 1:00 p.m. and without warning, Msg. Spiers, our principal, came on the PA system. "I want to inform the student body that John Kennedy, our President, has been assassinated." That was it; no speech, no condolences, no support for the student and staff. Nothing about this being a most tragic hour for all Americans. Most of us were speechless. Here's the first Catholic President, the youngest, and a hero to most of us, and now we're hearing that he's dead. Killed by a madman's bullet. Sadly, my Latin teacher, who was from the East Coast, was a cousin of the Kennedys. She was remarkably upset, and I felt so very sorry for her and her family.

I remember that evening well. I think it was a Tuesday, and I took off on my bike to meet up with a few of my friends down in old Arlington. I caught up with Billy, who was a year younger, and Pat, who is the one who almost died on New Year's. We just rode around in the rain and the dark and smoked a few Winstons. We stopped out in front of Cozey's house, thinking that we may stop by, but then we decided that it was not a night for socializing. Billy finally was the first to say, "Isn't it strange that here we are, just going on about our lives, and our country doesn't even have a President…"

Little did we know that Johnson was probably on that infamous flight where he would be sworn in as the next President of the United States. It would never be the same. Kennedy, good or bad, was still an icon. He brought respect to the Office of the President. He and his young family were perfect for the idealism that held America together. He had handled crisis well, and now he was dead. The days and weeks to come were somber. Billy, who was an up-and-coming vocal music star, who lived alone with his mother, asked me if I wanted to spend the night at his house and do some jamming. I declined. There was a hollowness in my heart that I didn't understand, and I felt very sad. I declined, even though I wanted badly to connect with Billy musically, because he was a rising star and a good guy, but at the moment, I had to decline.

That Saturday, the Bombas were bowling, and Pat, Toots, Morales, Kat man, Gary, and I hung around the bowling alley to eat and play the pinball machines. We used to play electronic baseball, because we had discovered that on the bottom side of the machine was an 'on' and 'off' toggle switch. As one of us played, if another stood alongside the machine, if an 'out' was hit, then if you quickly turned the machine 'off' and then back 'on', then the out would not be scored. We could play limitless games, all for just 25 cents. What a deal! Well, right above the arcade game was a mounted TV set, so as we played baseball, ate hamburgers, took turns manipulating the game machine, we would also watch 'Kennedy' specials on TV. In those days, we really only had three channels to choose from. Usually, the programming was very similar. Well, it was all news and replays of Kennedy's assassination. All of a sudden, we were getting a live feed from Texas as Lee Harvey Oswald was going to be transported somewhere. We stopped playing baseball, stopped eating, drinking, and all stared at the set, because we wanted to see this creature who had killed our President.

Well, it only took seconds, but all of a sudden, there was some sort of melee and struggle. I think that I remember two loud bangs, and Oswald crumpled. A man in a hat was restrained, and before we knew it, Lee Oswald was reported as being shot. Then he was reported as dead. Our reactions were mixed. Why was he in the open? Why didn't he have a bulletproof vest on? Who is this new assassin of assassins? What the hell is going on America? In the world? Conspiracy became the new word or the new generation.

Well, we would hear and view analysis of the Kennedy assassination for years to come. What always stood out in our minds, as youth, because we were all too familiar with the 6.5 mm Italian rifle that reportedly killed Kennedy in a moving car at more than one hundred yards, and he was hit several times. We all new this gun, because it and so many other pieces of post war trash were for sale via magazines at the time for about $29.00–$49.00. There's no way! As teens we knew what the 6.5 mm could do, and a bolt action military weapon was not going to perform like a 700 Remington. Bullshit was being handed to the American people, and we as emerging adults, could smell the stink.

Guns, bands, beer, parties, hyper-socializing, fast cars and girls were the focus of all of our activities. There was no element of being dazed and confused as we moved through the vacuum of high school. For us, there was no hockey, soccer, dance team, or any other distractions that would take away from our primary commitments. Interestingly, especially in comparison to the dealings of the present, at Upper Arlington, the home of the Golden Bears, throughout the 60s and 70s, there was a Sportsman's Club. Yes, this involved shotguns, bringing guns into schools, fishing, hunting, and all of the things that were necessary parts of American culture, since we were only one generation away from the farming, hunting and gathering culture of our grandparents. Most of us got BB guns, pellet rifles and even .22s for X-Mas by the time we were 8th or 9th graders.

Like in the movie 'The Christmas Story', a true classic, equal to Ben Hur, West Side Story and other media greats, getting a firearm was part of the culture. We also carried a knife, and that carried over well into the 80s and 90s. When I was getting employee awards via the public-school system in the late 80s and 90s, both times I chose an engraved hunting knife with a 4.5-inch blade and leather case. Today, that same tool would land a staff or classmate in jail awaiting prosecution for a felony. Society hasn't progressed or gotten more civilized, it has actually regressed, and fear influences all of the public sector's decisions.

Recklessness was a dynamic of our growing up. Drag racing on High Street, drinking to excess, random and unprotected sexual encounters, and even firearms would influence our lives. There was a Sunday, prior to us being drivers, when John's brother Jim picked me up in the middle of the afternoon. His convertible was filled with a bunch of my Watterson classmates, and we were headed to their estate out in the country. Jim had the top down, and I think that he may have been drinking.

We shot out onto Route 33 at over 100 mph, and his driving was frankly scaring the shit out of me. He weaved through traffic and passed when we had the yellow line. It was a damn scary ride, but I guess that I just 'let go and let God...' There are far too many times in life when shit happens, and we have no control over the outcome. This was one of those occasions. So, I 'just went along for the ride'! I also bitched at him several times to slow down, but he didn't respond. In fact, I think that he sped up just to be oppositional to my pleas. When we got to the main house, thankfully, we were all intact.

We were all grabbing beers and talking about going out for some shooting, Greggo, John C. and John's brother, and I were at the gun cabinet by the fireplace in the living room. Jim, who I still think was drunk, opened the case, pulled out a SW .357, cocked it, and pointed it directly at me and said, "You were worried about my driving? Shit, I could kill you right now!" Just as he said that, the gun went off with a great explosion. The bullet smashed into the marble fireplace and blew rock shards all over the place. The noise just about blew out my eardrums. When I was hit by the marble, I frankly thought that I had been shot, but luckily, that was not the case. Jim sheepishly dropped the gun and left the room. To this date, I do not think that since then, I've not seen that asshole again. I would bet that he went on to a life of being a chapel type, fucking little boys and guys, and living a reckless, spoiled life, but hey, what do I know!? What a queer dumbass!

This didn't stifle our connection with the country estate. It would stay as a gathering place for many months and years to come. During this time, I not only had my connection with Debbie from the north end, but her sister, who was in my class at Watterson, was taking a fancy to me. I had heard much about her, from a Watterson so-called tough, who had bragged about 'finger her' plus other things as well, so I thought that hook up with her may not be a bad idea. What I found, though, that during my freshman and sophomore years, that I had a degree of performance anxiety. I needed to venture out and find some 'sure things'. My buddy Greggo had a North High girlfriend, and he would relate to me that she was more than willing to give, so I would hang at her place whenever I could.

Once, I hit on Laura, a large breasted, long-haired chick who was about 5'2". She and I hit it off, and we decided on Sunday to head out and hear the 5th Order, Billy's group. She and I teamed up with Greggo and Christie. We went to Laura's house after picking up Christie, and her dad was enough to put the fear of the Lord into anyone. He huffed and puffed about us going out, but she knew how to handle him. She just placated him as we prepared to leave, so off we went. Laura and I in the back seat and Christie and Greggo in the front. Well, we hadn't gotten too far before Laura got really frisky. She got sexually aggressive, and we got down to business, like now. I loved those 32 D tits, and she was giving me a hand job.

Well, we hadn't made it halfway to Country Dale, the concert site, and I had cum all over her. We hung together at the concert for a while, but when it came time to leave, great! We dumped her off, then Christie, an off we headed to High Street to drag race. Greggo always had large engine Buick's and Oldsmobile's, and we were great competition to the 289s, 409s, 327s and other hot rods on the main strip of the OSU campus. At that time, his 400 cubic inch Buick could kick most vehicle's asses. This always ended at a stop at the White

Castle, and we would get the standard, five burgers each, fries, and a coke. Delicious! A very healthy diet!

There were others, and for the life of me, I can't remember this little chick who I hooked up with, via the Christie connection from Whetstone. She was cute and petite, and we hit it off well. I would usually hook up with her following gigs that our band played. Our lead singer lived on the north end, and I usually dropped him off, then I would go to her house. However, during one encounter she kinda scared the libido out of me. We were really going at it in the back of my 1961 Falcon, and we were kissing, rubbing, grinding and touching just about everything there is on the human body.

As I slowly undressed her, and got her pants down around her knees, I asked her how far she wanted to go. Her response was, "As far as you want to go!" Damn! That's a lot of responsibility. I think that my biggest fear was, could I satisfy her? I wasn't worried about her getting pregnant or social disease, it was all about satisfaction. We never did get totally comfortable, so I settled for sucking on her barely findable nipples, fingering her tight little pussy and getting a rather rough and tumble hand job. I don't remember ever seeing her again. I think that I feared that she wanted it all, and I wasn't sure that I had that to offer! At least not yet.

Well, girls would come, and girls would go. Many I met while playing with the band, mostly at Whetstone. We also did a lot of garage and basement gigs in Upper Arlington. Having rather long, curly, blond hair may not be as good of a chick magnet like a puppy is, but it sure helps. I always had a little Debbie to fall back on, but her and I just didn't have it going on sexually. I met one of her classmates at a dance one night, Lynn S. She had long blonde hair, a beautiful body, nice tits, a quirky personality and a large nose, but overall, she was a keeper. Our relationship, though, was either hot or cold.

One night, I was at her place in the north end, and I had hitched rides to get there, and her parents were gone. We eventually ended up in her bed and the bumping and grinding really got going. We had done quite a few shots before we got to making out, so her clothes came off easily. Man, did she have a bod! Firm tits, small waist, and soft, smooth skin. I figured that this was like Tony and Maria in West Side Story's moment of true love. As we got closer and closer to the main physical connection, she was wet, hot, and already thumping. She all of a sudden got squirmy on me. Her little pussy became a moving target, and she buried her head in the pillows.

Damn that superego! It was not going to be my night of sexual maturity. However, her body in and of itself was enough to turn anyone on and I remember cumming all over her stomach. This grossed her out, probably because she had never experience hot, smelly, body juices. She reacted with a 'yuck' exclamation, left the bed, and headed to the bathroom. Seeing Lynn after that became rare. We never got sexually friendly with each other again, and eventually, she went her way, and I went mine.

School continued to be a drag in my life and definitely a low priority. The work wasn't challenging, and it was overall too boring. I've always been amazed at the fact that most schools are based upon the same model of operation as any other school. Few, if any, ever breakaway and try to make the learning environment exciting and entertaining. Kids come to school for social reasons, but their reasons are mostly external to the core of the school day. Schools do little, if anything, to promote healthy social relationships, conflict resolution skills or just generally fun activities.

It's amazing how many students succeed in schools in spite of the inadequate programming and preparation that the schools haphazardly offer. Conversely, it's amazing how many brilliant students drop out of school, only to go on in life and become hugely successful people. I fell into the middle ground, whereas I basically bombed out of school, served my country, then jumped back into the system to get all the degrees necessary to go back into the educational inferno and make a difference.

Over the course of the past two decades, I have received three national awards for Developing Teen Leadership and Prevention programs, plus my work has been acknowledged at the state level repeatedly via awards and dozens of newspaper and magazine articles. I've had the pleasure of working with fine people like Suzanne Somers, Muhammad Ali, Jerome Bettis, Bill Sanders, Laurie Stewart, John Crudele, Milton Creigh, Rich Strenger and numerous outstanding educators and community members who want to see a 'difference' in how things are 'done' and 'run'. I concur. I've always felt that my Golden Bear years and experiences literally paved the way for me to be in successful professions.

Well, by the time the sophomore year was winding down, my future at the Watterson was questionable at best. Our band was now doing frat and sorority parties on the OSU campus and at the OSU student activity center, so hanging out with the big boys was getting to be the thing to do. These parties, although civilized to a point, involved a lot of booze and beer, and we would get in on it right along with those who hired us. What also became a bonus was, as the parties would wind down about midnight, the frat dudes always wanted a few more songs.

Well, it became 'pass the hat' time. This would usually double our income for the night, plus we'd get to suck down a few more beers. Killing brain cells and turning myself deaf over the weekends was not helping my school career, plus my cocky attitude was only getting worse as I could see that before too long, we, as a class, would be running the show.

I was hanging in the hallway after lunch one afternoon, along with my buddy Phil. He's the one with the lesbian mom. We were at the drinking fountain, and here came Father Durban. Holy shit! Well, right away, his voice goes up to about 30 decibels and he's ragging on us about getting a drink and not being in class. Well, I bent over to get a drink, and I tried to explain to him that I was thirsty. Just then, the bastard hauled off and cold-cocked me in the jaw with his first. Shit, my mouth was open, and all I could think was that he broke my jaw. Enough! I cold-cocked him back, and he slammed against the lockers, and then Phil intervened. That incident got me suspended, grounded, beaten with a belt and my conduct score dropped to 65 out of 100 for the marking period. I was in deep shit, but I'd seen and experienced too much abuse at this school, and over the years in the Catholic schools, and it all of a sudden wasn't going to encroach on my life. Bullshit!

One day, in Religion Class, where all we did was read the Bible, this crazy-ass assistant pastor from St. Christopher's parish just jumped up out of his seat, stopped what we were doing, and proceeded to call this one kid to his front desk. He yelled at the kid for having too long of hair bangs and proceeded to get out a pair of scissors and cut them off. Damn! Well, one of the kids finally got him back, because on another day, in the early fall, this kid was resting his head on his book, and Father jumped up and ran down to his desk and swiped his book. He opened it up, and all of the center pages of the book had been cut out and there was a transistor radio in the book. Genius! Hell, the kid should have been referred to MIT, but no. Forkamp, I think was the sadist bastard's name, told the kid that by Monday he would have to copy by hand, pages 101, 102, 103 and 104 from the Columbus phone book. Now, I came from the land of having to memorize dictionary columns, being hit by recess bells and copper rulers, which was excessive and downright mean.

Well, it was Monday before we knew it, and we all couldn't wait to see if this guy got his punishment finished. We had guessed over the weekend that this could be as many as 10,000 names, addresses, and phone numbers. We sat in class, and we were off again having someone read the Bible to us, then some Judas bastard spoke up and asked father if so-n-so had turned in his punishment. Forkamp, who was always loud, yelled out, "That's right! Mr. Radio needs to turn in his phonebook assignment."

At this moment in time, everyone kinda held their breath. The kid got up, opened his folder, pulled out a bunch of lined legal paper, and headed to the front of the class. He laid the assignment on the priest's desk and turned to walk back to his seat. All of a sudden, Forkamp let out with a roar, "What the hell is this?" The kid slowly turned and said, "It's the assignment that you gave me. Pages 101, 102, 103 and 104 from the Columbus Phonebook." Forkamp looked at him with a stare that would melt metal, but he remained silent for what seemed forever. "Well, I didn't say that you could do the yellow pages!" The kid responded, "No, Father, you didn't say that I couldn't either!" Case closed.

I'm sure that the kid would have to deal with some pretty serious paybacks. It was worth seeing this abusive Aquinas throwback meet his match. He had a reputation for being sadistic and abusive and totally unreasonable. This was a good lesson for him, but we all doubted if he had any capacity for learning how to interact with the students in a humanistic way.

There was another classless maneuver by a priest named Joe Ewald. He too had a rather mean streak. There were days when he was okay. One day, he called a guy named Mike up to his desk and asked him to remove his 'dickie'. These turtleneck concoctions, that only had a neck piece, were becoming very popular, mainly because they helped to keep you warm in our cold school, but in an all-boys class, to ask a teen to remove his 'dickie' was just not a bright move. In the back of class, near where I sat, Tim D. and another guy were laughing so hard that their desks actually tipped over.

Now, these were the kind of desks that you could only enter from one side, and as fate would have it, both of them fell so that they now were stuck in their desks. This even got the class in more hysterics. Well, Ewald wasn't going to have any of his nonsense. He came storming down the aisle, slapping his way at all of us, and then he got to Tim and this other guy. He grabbed each of them by the ear and literally tried to pull them back up by their ears! Damn! Ouch!

Call F. Lee Baily, this is fucking torture and abuse! Well, Ewald almost fell down on top of both of them.

Rumor was, all the while this was going on, Mike, the dickie man, left the room. He came from a very well-off family, and he went to the payphone to call home and get some legal advice. Good for him, because even if he lost his dickie, he had balls! Father Ewald could not manage the situation, so he finally backed off and let the guys get back up on their own. Then he started this sissy slapping each of them. It pissed me off just to watch. I felt like decking the bastard where he stood, but I cooled it, because I realized that it was not my fight. It was bullshit, and I didn't like the stink. My days at Watterson were now quickly coming to an end. I was determined to make it happen. The good news was, Mike, the dickie man, ended up retaining his right to wear his dickie, after his father, who must have been a huge donor to the church, had called the Bishop's Office. Case closed.

Well, by the close of the sophomore year, I had gotten two grading periods of a 65 out of 100 or less in conduct, so by the rules of the school, I was out. My dad had grown up with and gone to school with Monsigner, and when I arrived home on Friday, my dad was there, and he advised me that I would be enrolling in Upper Arlington High School on Monday. The deal that had been cut with his childhood friend, classmate, former seminary chum, now turned total asshole, was that I was being transferred based upon the family's choice to have me closer to my home, so that I could walk to school. No discipline records would transfer. This was a very happy day, because now I was 100% Golden Bear. However, rumors would fly, and I thought that I'd just keep reality to myself.

Enrolling at UAHS

Monday arrived in no time, and the deal was, until I got placed in UA, I was grounded. So, my weekend was boring, to say the least! Toots picked me up in his 406 Galaxy, and off we went to the land of gentry. I reported to the office and was greeted by the Asst. Principal, Dave. I'd heard rumors that he and his secretary Katie were having an affair, but I figured that was his and her business; however, it was intriguing information. He greeted me with a "So, you're Thom…" He went on to tell me he knew of our family and the family business and what houses he knew that had been built with 'our' lumber. He was even aware that the Galbreath Mansion on Scioto Country Club had many of its materials supplied by the family company. All I could think of was this guy must be some ass-kisser to know that. Then again, the more he knew, the better off he was as far as dealing with discipline.

Dave was quick to tell me that there was an 'ugly rumor' going around that I had been kicked out of Watterson. I didn't even acknowledge that statement. He then took me around, showed me the setup of the school, explained the dress code, and reminded me that my hair had to be a certain length. He then dropped me off to the guidance counselor to get a schedule. All the counselor could do was relate each course that he was enrolling me in as to how this would help me when I went to OSU. I finally told him that I had no immediate interest in OSU, and I was undecided as to what I wanted to do after high school. We concluded our conversation with him reminding me that when the time came, I would sign up for military draft via his office. This was unsettling, because the French had pulled out of Dutch Indochina, and now the country was called Vietnam. American troops were starting to be sent there as 'advisors'. Bullshit! Big Brother was slowly planning something, and the more you learned, the more you realized that the shit was going to hit the fan worldwide. It was just a matter of when. I left the counseling office, which was a complete misnomer, because there was no 'counseling' going on in these offices. It was just a paper-pushing gathering of adult advisors who wouldn't have a clue how to deal with something psychological in nature. Now I had a schedule; there were only a few weeks left in the school year, and nobody, within the ranks of the teaching staff in particular, even knew that I'm there! I went straight to the library where I ran into my best childhood friend, Gary, and he was flanked by two chicks. One named Cindy and the other Sue. I knew of Sue, because not only was she a complete knockout, but she also had a reputation of dating some of the super studs from both Arlington and Watterson.

I was amazed when she gave me some pretty serious stares and smiles. However, I was the new flavor of the week, so I guess I slowly recognized that I was to draw attention. Classmates, who were friends, would seek me out to say hi. Other classmates, who learned of my presence, would find me to see what I was all about out of curiosity. Then there were those who would seek me out because of a certain reputation, to see if they might want to consider trying to kick my ass. If they thought that they could, I knew that they might go for it, because it could lift their reputation. Luckily, I had good relationships with some of the upper classmen, some who were tougher than shit—Tony S., in particular, who was cousin to many of my buddies, including Gary, Mark and other Italians who I hung with as a junior. At about 180 lbs. and 5'9", he was by far the toughest guy I've ever known. He could take out anybody.

I took my time finally arriving at classes, but within the week, I had landed in each and every class. In P.E., it was the conditioning and wrestling rotation. The P.E. teacher, who was a prick named Marv, was quick to tell me that I was at Arlington because I thought that I was a tough guy. He said, "We'll see. I'll put you up against some of our toughest and see how well you can wrestle." Well, I really wasn't out to prove anything. Frankly, I wanted to steer clear of trouble, because like my entry into Watterson, I was more or less on probation, and I couldn't let trouble find me. Marv was out to just set me straight and possibly try to humiliate me. My day came to wrestle, and it kinda became the talk of this 90-pupil class. Marv had me matched with Gary S., who had a reputation as being tough, quick tempered and also deeply in puppy love with Sue, who he had heard was now looking to score with me. So, he had a lot at stake here. His reputation, his needing to put me in place and a need to be the dominant male, so he could go after the prize pussy in the school. He was also a guitar player in Billy's band, and he knew of my skills and Bill's desire to possibly get connected with me musically. That would mean his demise! Fuck, I was teetering on a possible disaster.

It finally came time to wrestle, and luckily for me, this was a major force in my life. All of the push-ups, weightlifting, boxing and other training were going to help me immensely. Frankly, when our match started, surrounded by a gigantic loud crowd, I was surprised that Gary was lacking in the upper body strength department. I was able to bring him down and subdue him in mere minutes. It took about three falls, and finally, I was able to pin his long-haired ass to the mat. He was squirmy, but not a match for a guy who had fought and trained as a fighter and also had a tremendous amount of adrenaline and testosterone. After this, we became 'talking friends' but other than that, we just went our separate ways. In the days and weeks to come, if I was asked once or a thousand times, "So, I heard that you kicked Gary's ass. So, how'd you do that?" I never really responded. I just smiled. Trouble always breeds trouble!

My matriculation to UA and the life of the Golden Bears was short. School was getting ready to dismiss for the summer, and it was time to start planning our free time. Unfortunately for me, I was faced with summer school. I was lacking in language credits, so my folks signed me up to take Latin. What a drag; having to get up each morning for six weeks and go learn a language that has no real use was frustrating. I always wanted Spanish, because it's used in our culture, but my keen witted academic advisors always scoffed at the idea. They said that Spanish was for those who wouldn't go to college. Go figure! Ignorance and lack of foresight is sad.

By the Dashboard Lights...

Our band was doing well, and we were preparing for a summer of fun and many gigs. One thing that I started noticing was that many times each day, a cute, dark-haired brunette and usually another girl would cruise by my house, honk, and keep going. One night, very late, I was coming home from a party with my little Debbie girlfriend. The cruising Comet came to a stop. It was foxy Sue and her buddy, Cindy. They talked for a while and then left. After I was in the house for a while, Sue called on the phone. We ended up literally talking for hours. It was obvious that she wanted to hook up, and I finally got the courage to ask her out. We agreed to go to the outdoor picture show. Man did the word spread about this. I got all kinds of questions from friends. "Hey, what's up with you dating Sue?" I would just say hey, we're going to a movie, that's all. Plus, I had to hide my tracks from Debbie, so that she didn't know that I was going out on her, behind her back.

The date with Sue went great, and I had never smelled a girl that had such a sweet fragrance. She was beautiful, petite, sexy, and sassy. She had a nice ass that drew attention as she walked by people. We spent a lot of time together during the first few weeks of summer, and we started to get pretty hot and heavy as we made out. One night, when we were out with Cindy and Dave, we were down at Griggs Dam on the Scioto River. We had blankets, and each couple found a nice, discreet piece of lawn to lay on and make out. That night was a whole new introduction to getting hot. I got in Sue's pants, and she was hot and wet and humping as I slid my three fingers in and out of her. She latched on to my pecker and stroked it ever so slowly, until I came like I had never come before. It hurt, because it felt too good, and she still wanted me to keep stroking her as we talked about just how serious we were with this relationship. Then, finally, I got the nerve to ask her just how far would you like to go? She replied with hesitation, "All the way…" You can bet that within a day, I was down at the gas station by the river, buying condoms and figuring where she and I could go to make love.

Well, we found all kinds of places. One of our sexiest encounters was in Cindy's back-screened porch, late one night, following one of our band gigs. Sue told me that she would be spending the night at Cindy's, and I just said that I'd stop by once we got done with our frat party. We agreed to meet on the back porch, and if I remember right, Cindy's dad and stepmom, who she lived with, were out of town. When I arrived, it was late; very late. I was almost hesitant to try and muster her. As I entered the house through the back-porch door, Sue appeared almost immediately. She had a blanket around her, and immediately we started making out in an intense way. We dropped to the glider, and the blanket slid back off her shoulders. She had on a cute little sleeping top with short shorts, No bra, and a very warm body. We mashed like at no other time.

As I slid my hand onto her breast, her nipples were firm, and she got more excited. She unbuttoned my jeans and reached in for my hard, hot, throbbing cock. I then moved my hand down to her pussy, and she was wet and hot, so we spread the blanket out over the glider. I slowly removed her shorts, and I unbuttoned her sleeping top. She tugged at my jeans and tried to unbutton my Rolling Stones type shirt. Before we knew it, we were pretty much undressed and ready for some real loving. Entering Sue was a whole new experience. Warm, soft, slick and hot would best describe my initial reaction. Then, there were these lovely perky breasts to kiss, lick, suck and massage. We went at it like two lovers who hadn't had water in a month, who had just come to a waterfall. It was fantastic loving, and it set the stage for the next year or so to be just as good each and every time! We were falling in love!

Two-Timing

That summer, we had a lot of gigs up at the Whetstone Recreation Center. This really brought in the north end crowd, and my girl, little Debbie was always there as a groupie. Unfortunately for me, one night, when we were playing with the Dantes, a big-name group from Worthington, Sue and friends and little Debbie were all at the same dance. Somehow, and to this date I'm not sure how, but they connected. Probably because they were the two best-looking petite brunettes in the whole joint. So instead of fighting, they chatted. Well, mostly likely sooner as opposed to later, they discussed boyfriends and they both quickly realized that the curly haired guitar player on the stage is dating them both. Similar lines of bullshit and same places for parking and making out. Holy shit! I felt like a dog shitting razor blades when I got the news.

I got a call from Sue at about 2:00 a.m. She beat around the bush initially, but finally she cut to the chase. She and Debbie had talked, and I was the Schmuck of the Year. Now, it was my challenge to somehow save something out of all this. Well, it took hours, but before sunup, Sue was backing being with me if I cut all ties with Debbie. I agreed. I did let her know that out of respect, that I had to deal with Debbie directly to finish this. She thought that was okay. As the self-centered, living for the day, going-for-the-gusto Schmuck, I called Debbie and set up a date for that night. Considering that it was now about 8:00 a.m., she agreed, but she told me that she had met Sue the night before.

Well, I took her out to John's country estate to talk, plus I took along a couple bottles of Ripple. The wine loosened her up, and before I knew it, we were in the back seat. She was much friskier than she had been in the past, and I had her bra off and her pants around her knees in no time. Her pussy was hot but not sweet smelling like Sue's. It was obvious that she was willing to go to any lengths to keep me, so if fucking me was the answer, great! She just didn't have the libido, urge or whatever. The actions were there, but there was no sexiness. I went ahead and slid my cock in her, and I was amazed staring at her small tits with very dark, luscious nipples. Debbie was part Indian, so the dark pigmentation was a turn-on. She was pretty much a dead screw. There was cooperation but no passion. Lust was not in her heart. It was overall an encounter of the third kind, by the dashboard lights, but it had little, if any meaning. I eventually figured that it was probably like the relationship her dad had with her mother. He would just slam her down, fuck her, produce another kid, and life would go on. There was little or no passion. There was no real love. Sadly, it was time to bid farewell. She was cute as a bug's ear and had a body to match. She hailed from the other side of the tracks, kinda like 'Down in the Boon Docks'. She wasn't for me, and I just didn't want to use her any further. Time for me to get real and honest!

CRO Times

Fall was quickly upon us, and football tryouts were complete. I couldn't even walk on the field because the coach told me that I was expelled from Watterson and was not eligible until I had completed one year at UA. I'm not sure where he got his info, but to retaliate, I just told Marv that they would have had one of the Watterson's best and fastest talents, but they had already decided against that. God help their soul if he played them. He just gave me a stupid, jock-faced look and went about his business. He probably had to be naked to count to 21!

Invitations to join CRO came out in August, and we were supposed to meet at Jones's field on a Sunday afternoon. I was truly relieved when I got mine. If a person didn't, then you had to consider yourself a non-person, and you might as well have committed suicide or gone off with the Peace Corps and did animal husbandry studies with the folks in Africa. The rest of your high school time would be spent in seclusion and rejection. You would be treated as if you had the cooties. Whatever, were they?

It was a tremendous feeling to get your CRO shirt, pay your dues and know that when the parties started or if you needed backup, the CROs would be there. When one was attending a school with over 2000 students and only three grades, numbers meant everything! Our CRO numbers were huge, and we were intent on carrying on the partying and craziness of those who preceded us. The studs and hard bodies from the class ahead of us facilitated a smooth leadership transition.

Our parties started to switch to Murphy's Party Barn, which was way up in Worthington near Sawmill Road. This was a place where we held many of our drag races. Straight country road, no traffic, and some very fast cars were around in 1965. We were entering a new level of craziness. Besides the Party Barn, we were pretty much taking over Olentangy Inn, a motel near Scioto Country Club, which was very loose with its registrations. Parties there tended to be mini orgies, and they were very frequent. One night, someone brought a bitch they had picked up at the Thirsty I near the OSU campus. She was pretty well tanked, and she was loose. One by one, we made love to her, and to our amazement, she wanted more. Damn! Eventually, we ran out of guys, so my buddy Lonnie called the manager, who he had somehow connected with, and invited him down for some drinks and a fuck. Damn, this guy showed up with a bottle of wine, some flowers, and a hard-on. We had adjoining rooms, and we pointed him to the bitch in heat. Soon, he returned, looking rather distraught. He said that she would have nothing to do with him, and off he went. Holy Christ, who knows what he tried to do to her, because no one else had a problem. Easy in and easy out. He was a reject. So, when we checked out in the morning, she was left to fend for herself, but at least the bill was paid.

A formula started to develop as we became solid juniors, which would last almost until graduation. We lived life in the fast lane, racier than 90210, and more balanced than 'Dazed and Confused'. There were a lot of 'West Side Story' in all of us, because there was pride and togetherness in what we did, whether it was vandalism, drinking parties, gang bangs or straight up with your girl, or any other girl. There was a charisma of being like Zorro, definitely one of a kind! Plus, above all, there was dignity. If you picked a fight, or got in one, it was mono against mono. Weapons were never an issue. There was an exception to that, though.

Toni S., a buddy who was a year older than me, was pound for pound the toughest guy in much of Columbus. He was tremendously aggressive, and he didn't fear anyone. He could put a cigarette between his thumb and forefinger, and do a one arm, one leg push-up and put the cigarette in his mouth and rise back up to the starting position. He was a good guy to know. He could do that with either arm! Well, the story I got was, he had beaten some other tough's ass at a street dance, and this guy and his buddies sought retaliation. They somehow found out where Toni lived, scoped out his bedroom, and fired a single shot from a rifle through his window that hit his headboard. Toni cooled it significantly after that.

However, I did hear that he got in a fight during spring break of his senior year down in Daytona Beach and no one won; both just walked away. Then unfortunately, the following summer, Toni got his arm stuck in a cement mixer, which crushed his left hand. After the accident, I ran into him, and he had his hand surgically sewn to his chest as a way of grafting skin to repair his injury. His fighting days were pretty well done. His reputation still resonated for years.

The life formula became school, out on Tuesday, Wednesday and Thursday for band practice and party on the weekend. I used to even keep record of how much I scored with my girlfriend on my calendar! Going to school was just a thing that one had to do. I did enjoy Journalism and Sociology class, though. In Journalism, we could mostly do what we wanted, and so, my creative side would venture out. Writing a story for the school newspaper was like composing a song. So, it was fun, and it was a great learning experience.

In Sociology, the teacher got us into some pretty profound thought. When we read 'Black Like Me', he really opened up many false notions that we all had about blacks. As a class, we began to have a much greater appreciation for the huge amount of oppression that the blacks were experiencing since being brought to America. This I could really relate to being Irish Catholic. Most realized that the Irish were treated like crap when they first started entering the U.S.A. Plus, to date, many grown-ups had prejudices toward 'Mackerel Snappers'.

Art class had its usefulness, and the teacher wasn't much older than us. She was wired and a bit tight. Ohio driver's licenses were made out of paper in those days, and we spent many class hours working on altering the birth dates on our licenses for anyone who wanted a free ticket into the many bars along High Street in the OSU area. It was a pretty easy procedure, but it took teamwork to make it successful and look real. We'd first take an Exacto Knife and remove the layer of paper that had the last number in your birth year. For most of us, that was 9. We would then take chalk that was the same color of the paper, a medium tan, and smudge it on the place where the number had been removed. We'd do several licenses at a time, and then we gave them to Tanny, a very cute chick in our class, and have her take them to typing class.

She would then scout out the typewriter with the closest typeset to match the rest of the numbers on the license. Eventually, after much searching around, she found the perfect match in a typewriter that was in the yearbook and Journalism classroom. Perfect! She was such a star, and cute on top of it, so no teachers ever asked her profound questions like "What are you doing?" She just went about her business as she pleased.

When the licenses were done, she would bring them back and give them to Gary, Rick and me. We would lightly go over the numbers with light colored chalk again and place each individual license in an enveloped for delivery to the proper person. We'd instruct whoever was paying the $10 for the alteration to place the license in one of the plastic holders in a purse or wallet. These tend to blur the document somewhat and makes them look even more legitimate. Then the person with the new license had to go to the Secretary of State's Office and apply for a new license because they had lost theirs. This was a very productive venture, and it worked each and every time.

However, in the years to come, the Ohio Department of Motor Vehicles would put an insignia over the face of the license, and they eventually went to color and plastic. The license served its purpose of getting you into any bar, but you were restricted to 'low' beer only. Ohio and Colorado had 3.2% alcohol beer, and this was for the 18 to 20-year-olds. Then there was 'high' beer which interestingly was at best 5.0% alcohol. The reality was, you could get just as blitzed on 3.2% as any other beer. On the weekends, however, we would head to the ghetto and get Colt 45, because that malt liquor reportedly had the highest alcohol content of all beers.

If you were in the bars on the weekend, as it got late, and the bar was crowded, you could pretty much order what you wanted. We'd even do shots. I remember going to one sleazy bar with my buddy Greggo, because he said they'd serve us anything. Well, we sat in his smelly joint, drank 7 and 7s and listened to this new vocal artist on the jukebox. A guy named Diamond singing about 'Solitary Man'. It was a catchy tune, and I sure could relate to the words, but I just didn't see it as band music.

I ran into that art teacher one time when I was out selling magazines door-to-door. I actually came to the apartment where she resided. Strange to meet up eyeball to eyeball with your superior and she's wearing just a short bathrobe and looking mighty fine. Well, that went nowhere fast, and it was back to the regular grind. However, when we had our tenth reunion, I believe, she was there looking hot. I shot the bull with her, and she was very talkative. It seems that she got divorced, left teaching, and was making her way successfully in the business world. She kept asking me about my buddy Rick. She talked about writing to him when he was fighting in Vietnam and how she was looking forward to seeing him. Well, I hadn't seen him, and I was with a very hot date, so I moved on. I did run into Rick at a friend's condo about 2–3 days later. I asked him what was up with the art teacher, and he just smiled, chuckled, and said, "What a great fuck." I guess that she found him, and he then must have really found her! Cool! All of us had fantasies about doing certain teachers or substitutes, but most of them weren't attractive. So, I never had that opportunity as far as I remember.

CRO/ORC parties started being pretty regular, and those who were doing the planning definitely showed their business acumen with each and every event. They were all mostly keggers, and they even started adding food buffets to the parties as well as live music. There was always a cover charge, and we knew that someone was making some bucks off of these ventures, but we didn't care. The food was always catered by our favorite eateries. Tommy's Pizza, a landmark eating institution in UA, would have numerous pizzas for our consumption for a small price. There were burgers and fries from the Frech-o-Nette, a classy 1950s eatery located near the pool and Northern Park. A place kinda like the burger joint in 'Back to the Future'.

If I remember correctly, Fritch's Big Boy catered some great eats. There was also White Castle, the mainstay, cornerstone to any young man or woman's diet. White Castle wasn't exactly in UA, but their 5th Avenue and High Street locations pretty much had us surrounded. These parties had it all. Drinks, food and a rock beat. Our band only played at one or two of the gatherings, mostly because three of our band members attended Watterson, and there were always feelings that some drunk Golden Bear may use that as an excuse to escalate trouble at one of our CRO/ORC celebrations.

There was an unspoken exclusiveness to these parties, and everyone was expected to wear their proper CRO or ORC shirt, so it was easy to spot a party crasher. Plus, there was always a bouncer or two. Greg C. and Gus many times took on this responsibility, and no one wanted to cross their path without a smile. These guys were intense and a little crazy. They looked for trouble. Heck, one time we were up in Massillon, Ohio, the capitol of High School football. We were playing the Tigers, and this team historically were the state champions. However, this year, the Golden Bears were fielding a remarkably tough team. Greg came to the game dressed for war. He had on combat boots, a jean jacket, leather wrist guards, a heavy spiked belt and other tough guy attire. He literally went over the Massillon side of the field, displaying his CRO sweatshirt, and as nature would have it, he ran into his Massillon counterpart.

A tough black guy who was gutsy enough to confront Greg's obvious intimidation. Well, it got ugly fast, and suffice to say, regardless of how tough Greg thought he was or wasn't, he got hammered quickly. He was too far from his home environment, which housed one hell of a lot of pansy-ass white boys, to realize that in the working-class town of Massillon, everybody is tough. Shit, the City Council gives every newborn boy a football as a gift upon birth! The police broke up this melee, and they quickly escorted Greg to the gate. He was out! The Golden Bears ended up beating the Massillon dynasty. Getting out of town in one piece was going to be a challenge. The players bus and the spectator buses of Upper Arlington literally got peppered with rocks, bricks, stones, and God knows what else, probably even shit! There wasn't a window left in any of the vehicles.

Frankly, it was a scary thing to watch and be part of. We had driven a car, so we were able to basically sneak out the back entrance and get the hell out of dodge without having to run the gauntlet of attack. Cus, who was also called Cussy, was always teamed up with Greg. He and I had grown up together, and he was always a big, tough, fun-loving guy. He smiled a lot, and he was a good guy to have as a friend. He could also turn tough very quickly. He was a good balance for Greg. Cus was much more grounded in reality. When conflicts were initiated, he didn't always jump in with an attitude that he had to kick everyone's ass. He also wasn't out to kill his adversary.

I was at one of the CRO parties at Murphy's, with a new girl that I was hooking up with named Lynn. Sue and I were having some sort of falling-out, and Lynn had shown up at a couple of our band gigs, and she was petite, cute and hot. Lynn made for a good fill-in date. Well, a sophomore classmate, who was our age and was obviously held back at one time or another, was at the party too. He wasn't a CRO, but he knew enough of the longtime class members that no one paid it any attention. He approached Lynn and I and then I saw him putting a lip lock on her. Damn, I went after him like peanut on butter. I put a C-clamp on his throat and backed him up against the wall. It took a few moments, but I finally collected myself. Shit, what was I doing? He quickly explained in a quivering voice that he had known Lynn for a long time and that they used to date. I just told Price, back off, those days are past. He did. Whew!

The ARC, or Arlington Recreation Center, was one of our main hangouts. One Saturday, I was there playing pool and just bullshitting with my buddies, and here came a gang from the Grandview area. John R. was leading the pack, and I knew him from Watterson, where he had been expelled a few years back. He and his buddies and my group would all sneak into the Boulevard Movie Theater on the weekend. He had a little brother called 'potato bug', which I thought was one heck of a strange nickname. John was tough, but he was also a lot of hot air. He came from a rough, fighting kinda family, so he was someone who had to be reckoned with. John had a bunch of other greasy-haired roughnecks from Grandview with him, so it didn't look like this was going to have a happy ending. In these moments, I always felt rather torn between my St. Agatha, Watterson vs. Upper Arlington, Golden Bears mixed allegiances. So, I decided to take the initiative and went outside to try and head this group off. I noticed that they also had a carload of characters out on the street.

John and I engaged in conversation immediately. He started asking about the 'CRO gang'. He said that one of his 'boys' was beaten up 'by them CROs' the night before. Talking with John was never easy, because his breath smelled like that of a dead horse, and he spit as he talked with you. He also wasn't the sharpest knife in the drawer, so getting him to understand something wasn't always easy. He was unfortunately cursed with a weak mental and dysfunctional constitution. If he were in school 'nowadays', he would definitely be riding on the short bus. I tried to set him straight and told John that CRO was just a party group, nothing more. It wasn't a gang that was trying to control turf. Then he started asking about 'Tony'. *Shit*, I thought. *If you run into Tony, God help you.*

It was obvious that John was there in an attempt to elevate his reputation. He was dumb enough to think that if he could beat up Tony, then he could walk on water in his neighborhood. He was bright enough to know that Tony's reputation was just as strong in Grandview as it was in Arlington and elsewhere. Tony was Italian, and in Columbus, most of Grandview's residents were Italian. They were a very close-knit bunch of great people. John was too stupid to realize that if he did beat Tony, there would be 5–10 guys gunning for him within days. Every tough Italian in Columbus would be hunting his ass down. Guys like Sean Kelleher, Frank Strange, and other toughs would be on his ass like stink on shit. Let alone the UA toughs would be wanting to avenge any CRO loss.

Well, he cooled it at that moment in time, but he wanted to set up a gang fight right behind the ARC. I told him that I'd pass along the information but to be aware that the CROs may not show. This was not their thing!

The exchange with John took place on Saturday afternoon. The word got out quickly on more than just both sides that trouble was brewing in Upper Arlington. What complicated this for me was that the Watterson crowd were somehow now plotting to have it out with the Upper Arlington CROs. Lucky for me, I talked with Dave, Jim, John and Greg, the Guise Band members, and we were booked for the following weekend. Knowing that many of these school verses school clashes usually came to critical mass very quickly, the upcoming weekend would be the most likely. John, our drummer, also shared with me that since all three schools—Upper Arlington, Watterson and Grandview—all had home games on Friday night, which would probably be D Day.

John's older brother was Frank. He was about 2 years older than us, and he had the reputation of being the toughest guy on the north end of Columbus. That account was probably true. I knew guys that he had clocked, and they had huge reputations for being tough. Well, Frank was feeding information to his younger brother John about what was going to go down. It really started to sound intense, because now, there was even talk of weapons. Not guns, like in today's world, which is the first line of offense by the assholes who rape, pillage, rob, and attack others. It would be West Side Story kinds of stuff. Knives, baseball bats, chains, brass knuckles, trash, rocks, and old-fashioned fists and feet. The latter were becoming extremely popular, since the boys from the hood would just as soon kick you in the balls instead of punching you. When guys would spar just for the fun of it, it was almost becoming an art form if you had great kicking abilities. Plus, you added to it the knife-like toe shoes made by Flagg and Richmond Bros., and it was something you had to know how to defend against. The thought of deflated nuts makes every guy sweat, then and now!

Our band was playing at a frat party on Friday night, and we were out of town at some party barn. Word did get out, mostly over WCOL, the rock station of Columbus in those days, that the police had intervened on a huge gathering of youth in the area of the ARC in Upper Arlington. The report stated that as many as 1,000 youth were turned around, searched, and escorted out of the small suburb by the police from the surrounding area. The Citizen Journal even had a small front-page article on the incident the following morning. The article said that various clubs, baseball bats, chains, and other so-called fighting paraphernalia was confiscated. No injuries were reported. However, by Saturday afternoon, I was hearing other accounts. My buddy Jon, who had transferred over to UA from University High School, had gotten into a fight outside the ARC with Lee. The story I got was Jon was quite drunk and had a run-in with Lee just outside the entrance to the ARC. Lee was several years older than us, a high school dropout, heavy boozer, and spoiled rich kid, who drove a brand-new 409 Chevy Impala. Tits car! I guess that he and Jon really collided hard, and Jon took a punch to the face that split his lips. His injuries were significant enough that he had to go to the hospital and get sewn up.

CRO parties and other CRO/ORC activities started to wind down for a spell. We all concentrated our efforts on planning our socializing and social acting-out at the Olentangey Inn. We also had a few other motels, closer to OSU campus, which started to become hot spots for fun and action. Plus, we still had basically unlimited access to John's parents' and grandparents' estate way out on Route 33. So, we always had some great options. The only problem with all of this was how we were quickly becoming prisoners of our own limited ability to make choices that included healthy choices in balance with the unhealthy ones we usually made. Plus, we kept living for the moment, and none of us were examining short or long-term consequences for our poor choices.

I remember one night, reading in a Saturday Evening post, an article that basically dealt with the emerging epidemic of teen drinking. It pictured a carload of teens in a convertible, chugging beer. I could all too well relate to that picture. It made me feel cool at first, thinking that we too, over the Midwest shared the same common bond to partying as these teens that lived somewhere else. After I re-read the story, I also felt rather scared. My dependency on alcohol and how it had become the common bond to my teen community left me shuddering.

The CROs weren't friends, and neither were my buddies from Watterson and elsewhere. They were just drinking partners. The glue that bound us was all primal and based on immediate gratification. The reality of the denial of our culture was now becoming all too evident. I was ready to break the mold and make some life-changing moves. Hell no, I didn't have the intestinal fortitude to do that. It was still far too important to be accepted, to be considered cool and to basically 'fake' having it all together. If anyone tried to attack, challenge, or pierce that bubble of narcissism, then I had to be inclined to stifle them by kicking their asses or harassing them to the point that they just socially vanished.

Getting Wild

Outside of the CRO world, we had activities, but all mostly were in the category of unhealthy or illegal. Gary and Gary, Alf, and I hung out a lot. Alf lived down by Jack Nicklaus, so he was in the big-time neighborhood. We'd often end up at Alf's house, and it was a do-as-you-please joint. His mother was a total alcoholic, to the point that she would drink vanilla extract if she was low on booze. Her husband was usually absent. He was a small-framed, carefree person who really never said much about anything. Alf had an older brother named Myles, who drove a totally cherry '57 Chevy convertible, floor shifter, 327 cu in engine, metallic blue, white interior and top, headers and a race cam. This car was well known as a street ass-kicker. There was a younger brother, confined to a wheelchair because he had been run over by a bulldozer at a nearby construction site. We had heard that the family received a $175,000 settlement for the accident, which would have explained why nobody worked. Sadly, the younger brother had some real psychological issues.

Gary and I arrived there one afternoon, and he was throwing everything he could grab around the kitchen. He was tossing pots and pans, bottles of ketchup, sacks of flour, you name it, and it came flying at you. Alf, Gary, and I tried to negotiate a truce with him, but he only escalated. Alf's mom was on her daily walk to the Tarpy Grocery Store to get a bottle of wine or whatever her pleasure was for the day. Half of the time, she just had on a house coat with nothing on underneath. She was a pathetic person.

We finally just moved ourselves downstairs in this tri-level home and let Alf's younger brother continue his rage. Alf shared with us that this was a common occurrence and that for half of the year, his brother was placed in a 'home' outside of their residence. In the lower level, Alf had his own private room, and he showed us what he had been working on. He had his mother purchase salt peter and the rest of the ingredients to make gun powder. He was working on a rather large bomb. It was probably in about the 5 lb. class. Whew!

He had even taken shotgun shells, split them open, removed the smokeless powder, and added this to his explosive concoction. Now, we had all been making various rockets over the years, but not bombs. Usually, we would go to the hobby store at Lane Center and purchase CO2 canisters. We emptied the gas, put the small cylinder in a vise, secured it, took a 10-penny nail, and knocked out the small end. Then, very carefully, we'd stuffed the tube with the heads of matches. It would take numerous packs of matches, and the job was tedious, but the final product was impressive. At the hobby shop, we would also get a supply of Jet Tex fuse, which was used to ignite the rocket.

At Northern Park, on the St. Agatha side, there was much construction going on, so we'd head over there to launch our rockets. Grady, Gary and I headed there on Saturday afternoon, and we had our super rocket that we were very excited to launch. We went to an area of a ton of concrete rubble were the former rectory house of the church sat. Now it had been demolished. We found a section of sewer pipe, about four feet long, propped it up with rocks, and slid the rocket into the lower end. All that was exposed was the end of the Jet Tex fuse. Gary came up with the idea that once we lit the fuse, if we blocked the backend of the pipe, then the rocket propulsion would help push it along. Sounded like a great idea. Now, on this sunny day, far across the field, about ¼ mile or so, there were slow-pitch softball games going on. We could just see the players and barely hear the noise of the spectators. Considering the distance between us, that wasn't surprising.

Well, it came time to launch, and Grady took the honors of lighting the wooden strike-anywhere match on his zipper, and then he touched it to the end of the fuse. Immediately, the fuse started smoking and hissing. The burning fuse kinda sounded like the fizz of an Alka Seltzer. It was slow to burn, and there seemed to be a lot of smoke from the fuse, a pause, and them *blam*! Whoa! That sucker was off so fast that you couldn't even see the projectile come out of the pipe. Then, within mere seconds, on the pitcher's mound, way—and I mean way across the field—*impact*! Damn, there was a cloud of dust and a whole lot of players scurrying about that softball field. We were like "Holy shit!" We were gone in a heartbeat.

All of us headed to my house, in the door, up the stairs, down the long hallway and quickly into my studio bedroom. We were laughing, bragging, and relieved that we didn't see anyone go down. Whew! This experience opened up a whole new line of explosive things that we could create. We did agree, though, that it would be down at Marble Cliff Quarry would be where we would launch these in the future. Not in areas where there were innocent bystanders within a ¾ mile of the launch site.

The following Friday night, with nothing much to do, Gary, Gary, Alf and I all gathered at Alf's house. Grady was out with Bev, or so we thought, so it was just the three of us. We played some cards and drank some beers at Alf's. Alf then started saying that his bomb was completed, and it was time to detonate this puppy. We were all like, hey, we're not crossing that rotten old trestle to get over the river to go to the quarry. Alf was like, hell, we'll just light it across the street, where the backyards are huge. So that is where we headed. Back behind Nicklaus' house and other prominent citizens.

These were all super ranch-style homes, 8,000 or more sq. ft. each. Each home had numerous sets of glass sliders that overlooked these huge backyards. There was a split cedar fence that separated the neighbors on the south from those on the north. Gardens were planted on both sides. We walked along the fence until we came to an isolated fence post that was hidden by ornamental trees or bushes. It had a flat top and was big enough to balance the size of Alf's explosive creation. The bomb was in a cube shaped container, with substantial fuse sticking out of the top. The fuse seemed remarkably short. You almost expected this puppy to be round, black, and have the word BOMB painted on the side, kinda like in the cartoons. This was one of Alf's things, so the creativity of shape was in keeping with the uniqueness of Alf as a person.

His real name was Bob, but everybody had always called him Alf. One thing we had all forgotten at this brief moment in time is that Alf ran the 440 yds. faster than anyone! He was reportedly the fastest guy in the county, but unable to make the track team because of his poor grades, attendance and age. He somewhere in time had been held back, so he was at least a year older than us. He was also so darn independent that it would be hard to believe that he could conform to the strict structure of an athletic team. Well, as not expected, Alf lit the fuse, and just about the time that he did, he was off, just as fast as the Road Runner! There was a brief pause. We all looked at each other with disbelief that there wasn't some sort of honorary announcement that it was time to light the bomb. When that hesitation dissipated, whoosh, we were off.

Gary, Gary, and I had barely rounded the side of one of the homes, and the blam from the boom of the bomb was more like '*ka-bam*!' One could hear windows break in the surrounding homes from the vibration of this combustible. This was an explosion that transcended our traditional little firecrackers, rockets, and fishing with M-80s and cherry bombs. This was one wicked device made from all-natural products. All I could think of was what ever happened to the first sap that mixed salt peter with charcoal and sulfur? Hell, he must have been turned into soup!

Before we knew it, we could hear sirens off in the distance, and so, we boogied to Alf's house, entered through the back, and headed down to his sanctuary in the basement. We were all panting like a pack of dogs that had been chasing a fox and lost the race. Alf was calm, cool and collected, and he wasn't even breathing hard. Alf lit up a cigarette, grabbed a Stroh's and sat down for some card playing. It took about an hour, but sure enough, there was a knock on the front door. Alf just said, "Ignore it." We did. Then there was a ringing of the bell and more knocks. Alt finally got up, looked pissed, and went to the door. Now, mind you, in the tradition of the Golden Bears, denial can also carry with it a huge amount of rage. When Alf answered the door, sure enough, it was a couple of police who were inquiring as to an explosion in the neighborhood. Well, Alf's defense was a very aggressive offense. He just lit into the cops, bitching at them like a raged beast. "Hell yes, I heard the explosion. Shit, it woke my handicapped brother! Why aren't you guys out trying to find who did this nonsense?" Alf came across so strongly that the cops just packed it up and left. It was obvious that they knew of the volatility of his household, and without any evidence, they just moved on. Great! Whew!

It took us days before we gathered up the fortitude to sneak over to the opposing neighborhood and check out the impact that Alf's bomb had on the surrounding area. Amazing! When we did see it, and it was late at night, but enough passive light from the surrounding estates lit up the backyards so we could see the devastation. Sure enough, the fence post was gone, and pieces were all over the place. All of the horizontal posts gone both directions, too, were scattered about. Remarkable! Then we got a "What the hell are you boys doing back there?" yell from one of the homes. Off we went, naturally with Alf far out in front. Back to his house we headed, in the back door, and to his place of safety. Soon, there was a ringing of the front bell. Alf assured us that whoever it was, would go away. No, they persisted, so Alf went to the door, all the while his mother, who was very tanked, kept yelling down from upstairs, "Who the hell is it? Send them the fuck away!"

Well, this time it was two detectives from the Juvenile Division of the UA Police Department. They knew Alf and the family well. One even stepped inside and responded to Alf's mom that everything was 'okay'. He went on to briefly explain that they were investigating a disturbance in the neighborhood. She replied with comments that sent the rest of us back down the lower-level stairs laughing so hard that we could barely contain ourselves. "Robert can help you catch those hoodlums. He's a good boy!" That was a powerful and distorted statement coming from a lady who looked like Woody Harrelson's lady landlord in Kingpin. Alf was pretty well-versed in how to bullshit and respond, so the detectives got nowhere fast. They did supposedly have some other shit hanging over his head, and they tried to use that as a lever to get Alf to have some ownership of the bomb incident. He didn't take the bait or the coercion. He blew them off and they left. It was easy to assess that he was going to be under careful watch henceforth.

Alf and a few others had been blamed previously for jacking beer out of the Nicklaus home, who lived one block over. The deal was, that when anyone of us or our buddies were caddying at Scioto Country Club, and Nicklaus, Walker Inman, the club pro, and guys from Sports Illustrated or other media were playing, then you knew that there would be a gathering at the Nicklaus home. That meant beer, and lots of it. It was always Millers', and there would be as many as ten cases at a time. Usually, Alf and big Gary would set up the heist. Alf, because of his cunning and speed, and Gary because of his brute strength. Thankfully, this entertaining took place frequently, especially as the Golden Bear himself lifted to stardom, so the Millers were always available.

This supplied Alf's place of sanctuary and allowed us refreshments when we were playing cards or just bullshitting. Thankfully, Alf's mom was never into beer, and I doubt that she even entered his private kingdom. Sadly, in the next few years to come, Alf got caught up in some sort of sting operation, that even included big Gary, and both were sent off to prison for many years. I believe that they were charged with the sale and distribution of marijuana. I heard that Alf got out of prison and was just absorbed into society. Gary got shock probation and moved to Florida. I've never seen either since those days of bombs and beers. Too bad, because Gary had been a close friend for many years.

Taking the Mask off

You know, during all of these teen times, everything wasn't about sex, beer, delinquency and just generally running wild. There were many years during our Golden Bear moments when we were just plain normal teenagers having fun. I remember one summer that I think big Gary and I fished in the Scioto River each and every day. We could drive, but without a car, bikes were our thing.

The river was not all that far from my house, so we'd usually just ride bicycles down to this ravine, head down the hill, follow the creek, go through the water drainpipe under the highway, and then appear over in Griggs Dam Park. Most of the time, we used cane poles that we hid in the woods near the river, and we could find our bait under the numerous limestone rocks that were on both shorelines. Crickets always worked best. We always caught a mess of fish, and it was usually a mixed bag of totally inedible carp, mud puppies, suckers, small mouth bass, needle-nose gar, and an occasional channel catfish.

When we got bored of the fishing, we'd always go looking for snakes. I had been a snake freak most of my life, but when they removed the woods behind St. Agatha to build a new church, I lost my place to hunt. Down at the river, there were many snakes. Some were downright mean and aggressive. I remember getting one banded water snake that had to be five feet in length. It was as thick as my arm. Every capture was always exciting, and usually, we'd just let everything go. One day, though, when we were catching really big crayfish, we decided to try and eat them. So, we built a fire, let it burn down to coals, and then dropped in the crayfish. When they were finally done, at least by our standards, we broke off the tails and tried these delectable morsels. Damn, they tasted like shit. No, they tasted like the river smelled! Horrible! They certainly weren't as delicious as the lobster that was grilled at home, usually on Friday's during Lent. Those were yummy!

One hot day, there were four of us hanging at the river. Tom, freckled Gary, Bonehead, and I. We were fishing a deep hole in the river, catching a ton of shiners and just having a lot of fun. Then Tom D. was asking me if I thought that Gary had freckles on his ass. I was like, "How the hell would I know?" Tom then had an idea. Now, this is 'Flubber Man'. Mischief was his middle name. He suggested that we all go swimming in the deep hole in the river. Why not, it was in the 90s, and we needed to cool down. So, off came the clothes and into the water we went. We were all pretty well hung the same, except Tom D., who was a year older than us and did have more hair on his body, but shyness was not an issue, and neither was penis envy. By the time you got into the cold running water, no one had a penis, or so it looked. They all shrank to about the look and size of an acorn top.

Well, Tom's plan was not only to verify if Gary had freckles on his ass, but to also take his clothes and split fast! We subtly told Bonehead of our plan, and while Gary was floating the rapids, enjoying his summer swim on one very hot day in central Ohio, off we went with his clothes. Shit, we were well on our way to the drain tube to go under the highway, and we could hear Gary yelling, "Come back, you bastards!" We didn't. We got to the ravine, headed up the hill, and then that son of a bitch, Tom D., wanted to throw Gary's bike down the hill, far into the ravine. "Hell no!" Both Bone and I said, "It's enough that he's naked!" So off we went, but we did drop Gary's clothes, piece by piece, as we went up Canterbury Hill Road. The last thing that I heard before we went our separate ways that afternoon was, "He does have freckles on his ass!" I think that came from Tom D.

Shooting BB guns and just being in the forest or the quarry became a regular activity for our small group, which quickly grew in size. Most of us had 1894-style BB guns, for which we had an 18-year-old whom we bribed to purchase them from the local hardware store for us. When we used 'real' guns, it was out at John's estate, and we just helped ourselves to what was in the gun cabinet—guns, shells and all. Our BB gun escapades were the most fun, because they did develop our marksmanship skills. We would perch ourselves on his old train trestle over the Scioto River and just watch and wait for turtles of various sizes, shapes, and kinds to come to the surface. Then *kerplunk*! We'd bang them with a BB that would just bounce off their shells. It was fun, though, and we were shooting at about 40 yards. Most of us got pretty deadly with our shooting capability, and so, we ventured out for more sporting game. On the property of the quarry, there were several old, deserted storage buildings. The windows were broken out, and lo and behold, these buildings were home to number feral pigeons. Well, one needed stealth to be able to sneak in and get a shot at roosting pigeons. You'd think that these unprotected, nuisance critters would be pretty dumb because they sure were in the city, but out in the desolate area of the deserted quarry, they were kinda smart. We got clever and savvy to their movements and behavior, and before you knew it, we were bagging warm-blooded animals. They only problem was, we didn't know what to do with them once we dropped a bunch.

Phil, one of my classmates from both St. Agatha and Watterson, got the idea that maybe some of the sucker fisherman along the river might want them. He said that these things are called 'squib' in diners. So, we gathered our kill and headed to the banks of the river where the wine-drinking sucker fisherman hung out. Holy crap, they gave us 50 cents for each bird, and one of them offered one dollar for each robin. He said, "The meat is so sweet!" We declined that offer, because we weren't into killing songbirds. It was kinda nice that our hunting adventure turned into a capital venture. It put us into an eight-pack of Stroh's, which topped off the afternoon well. Sitting on the trestle, drinking a cold Stroh's was kinda like the roofers in Shawshank Redemption. A man and his suds—it goes hand in hand with life.

The hunting, fishing and collecting of live reptiles and other critters really helped us to put life in perspective. In Golden Bear land, there was no connection to the natural world. We were only one generation away from the fields of farming, but everyone was depersonalized from the notion that something had to be killed so that you could eat steak. As burger joints started to surface, no one wanted to examine where this all fit into the food chain. It was not discussed, and it certainly was never part of our so-called sophisticated school curriculum. This was particularly interesting, because our next stopping point after high school was supposed to be Ohio State.

Upper Arlington, home of the Golden Bears built its reputation on exceptional sports programs and a high percentage of students finding academic success in spite of the educational program. In those days, the saying was, "You can attend OSU if you have a heartbeat and a diploma!" So very true! However, as the 'REGISTER HERE' for the draft posters became increasingly prominent around the guidance office, many of us were starting to face the reality that our future might reside in a rice patty in Asia as opposed to a coed dorm at OSU. Randomly, we were getting word of older brothers who were in Vietnam being sent home in a box. This was very alarming. I had one older brother return from Nam missing both of his lower legs. This was gruesome. Reality was slowly starting to seep into the land of 'everything is perfect, and all is well'.

Life Goes on

Well, the tough get going when the going gets tough, or so 'they' say. I've always wondered, just who in the hell are 'they'? Our band was gearing up to start adding new songs. It seemed that as more chaos in the world developed, with the fighting in Vietnam, in particular, there were also many integration issues with the blacks, and a man named Martin Luther King Jr. was trying to bring organized peace to the mess. We were reconstructing our song venue. The Rolling Stones, Byrds, Who, Ohio Express, and the Monkees were now influencing us more than the Kingsmen, Beach Boys, Yardbyrds with Eric Clapton, and The Beatles. However, The Beatles were in a transformation, and their music was being molded around responding to the social strife in the world and the emergence of a very strong drug culture. We still hung on to a few classics by lesser-known bands like the McCoys, Bobby Seger and Last Herd and individual performers, some of whom were making a real impact on the musical culture. Dusty Springfield, Carole King, James Taylor, John Denver and, of course, one who would become my favorite of all time, Janice Ian. However, she was only 15 years old at the time, and in my opinion, she was the most socially aware composer/performers of the 20th century. Her song Seventeen could be the theme song to this book. Later in life, I actually got to meet her. Very arrogant!

We continued to practice at a fairly regular rate, and it was usually at Jim's house. He lived next door to Pam, who went to Watterson. She hailed from what seemed to be a very well-healed family. She drove a brand-new Thunderbird. In spite of the nice car, nice house, and a fairly nice personality, she was thick and note cute. When we got a warm-up booking at the Sugar Shack on Summit Street, right on Campus. This was a great move for our future. The headliner was Bobby Seger, a newcomer from Ann Arbor. We all had our fake IDs for getting in. Playing and having a few brews was a cool way to spend a Wednesday, Thursday, Friday and Saturday night. Groupies are part of the band culture. You put a group of guys together, have them make a bunch of noise and somehow, out of the woodwork, here come the ladies. Well, as a rumor would have it, Pam, the Thunderbird girl, was hooking up with Seger. This I found to be very hard to believe. He was an emerging talent, fresh out of Michigan, who could probably have any chick in the house, and maybe he did. The rumor persisted about him hooking up with Pam. We let it go, because we needed to focus on our own issues. Getting the crowd primed before the big act performed was our challenge, and fortunate for us, it worked.

We weren't making much money, but we were building contacts, and that's what counted. When we were done, it was always exciting to watch Seger perform. I was amazed at the first time I met him, because for some reason, I thought that he'd be tall, kinda like the Motor City Madman, but he wasn't. He was compact and about my size. The man could belt out the songs. He could blend a blues quality, with soul and spirit into any rock n' roll song. To this day, I still go to his concerts, and I buy all of his albums, because he is the consummate rock performer. He delivers songs with a passion that is unparalleled to any of his contemporaries. Heck, Chevy still uses his vocals for selling their trucks. Like a rock. Bob is the rock of rockers!

Well, we moved on to other venues, and our music and even our clothes were changing. As the Byrd's sang, 'These times, they are a-changing' and they sure were. All of our hair was getting longer. Mine was curlier, and sandals often replaced shoes. One of our best jam sessions followed a trip the day before a hunt down in southern Ohio. We were asked to eliminate a bunch of rats that had taken up residence on Jim's grandparents' farm. It seems that both of his grandparents were placed in senior care centers, and they had a pretty substantial farm.

Well, Jim's dad brought us, plus about ten rifles and shotguns and a ton of ammunition down to the farm. He distributed the guns to all of us, showed those who had never shot, how to load, point and keep safe their weapon, and then we all headed down to the barn yard. There were about fifty big dog houses out in the yard. I guess that they had held sow pigs and their piglets, but they had all been sold at auction. The hog houses were supposedly overrun with barn rats. We were told that some were as big as cats! Jim's dad showed up riding a John Deere tractor, dragging a long chain. He pulled up to the first hog house, had us secure the chain around the structure, and lurched the house forward. Sure enough, rats scurried everywhere.

Those of us who knew how to shoot did, while the others just kinda looked with amazement. On the first flush, we tumbled about five rats. Damn! This was going to be one fun day. Well, we went through that barnyard, house by house, shaking out rats and blowing the shit out of them. Very disgusting creatures. None of them were much bigger than a fox squirrel. However, long teeth, a snake-like tail, and an evil look in their eyes put them damn low on the food chain. They are there somewhere near cockroaches, leeches and other scum sucking critters of the world. Frankly, this became a day of bonding for the members of the band and the others who tagged along.

What topped off the day was when Jim's dad and others were gathering up the fifty or so rats that we'd killed. Some headed down to the local mom and pop grocery store to pick up some drinks and treats. A day of rat hunting really takes it out of you. It was definitely a Miller moment! Well, my guys also scored on a gallon of moonshine for $10. That's a deal, if it doesn't make you go blind, cause your dick to fall off, or kill ya. Clear, colored booze just doesn't seem healthy!

The next day, we again were at Jim's, this time to practice seriously and work some of these new songs into our playlist. Heavy metal and psychedelics were emerging, and we had to stay current. Well, as we prepared to get tuned up and start rocking, we decided to get out the hooch and try it mixed with some root beer and a lot of ice. Damn, it looked harmless cause it was clear, but it tasted like Terpenhydrate, this disgusting cough medicine of the 50s and 60s. We continued to sip this shit, and after a drink or two, it wasn't all that bad. Several of us were sitting in the kitchen of this very open house. We were at the breakfast bar, drinking concoctions and tuning our instruments.

After about an hour, it was time for the band to get to the lower level of this tri-level and crank it up. Shit, when I started to move, I couldn't feel my legs. John, our drummer, was mumbling, as opposed to talking, and Greg our lead singer, was just about out of it. Practice, even if it went well, was going to be a bust, because no one would remember who played what and when. As Cheech and Chong would say, "This was some badass stuff…" I think that the remaining hooch became charcoal lighter fluid, because none of us were going to touch that shit again. Mixed or not mixed, no one's liver could handle too much of that poison. Plus, it had no 'girl' quality to it. Take that stuff on a date, give her a drink, and then you'd have to spend the rest of the night trying to get her sober. We still weren't sure if this shit would kill you or not. We planned to add songs like Paint It Black, 19th Nervous Breakdown, I Want to Be Free, 7 Plus 7 Love, Little Black Egg, Day Tripper, and others. So, this was exciting. Plus, we added the new version of Dancing in The Streets, which was great at either block parties, garage dances or frat gigs.

When we weren't playing, on the weekends, I now was spending more time with my buddy, Jon. He was a true party dude, and he lived in a household where there didn't seem to be much supervision or control. He and his brothers and sisters, more or less, did what they wanted to do. Jon spent a good amount of his free time working on constructing a dragster from a 1934 Plymouth Coupe. He had installed a Thunderbird engine in it. I believe it was a 312 cu in, with three duces, header, racing cam, modified intake manifold, and other go-fast adjustments. It had raised slicks on the back and smaller tires in the front.

He had a vision of when completed, it could kick ass on the High Street drag circuit. Every so often, we'd push it out of the garage, he'd start it up, and off he'd go. The mufflers had not been installed as of yet, so as he screamed through the neighborhood, it definitely brought a few people out of their homes to check on the commotion. One neighbor, who, I understood, starred in some TV show eons ago, would fly out of his house and come over to threaten Jon with the police. Jon would just calmly look at him and then tell him to 'fuck off!' Mr. Wendy's himself lived across the street, but he never said much. His daughters Wendy and Pam would sometimes come out to see the action, but other than that, only the former film star would raise a stink. Nothing was going to stop Jon from doing what he wanted to do. He continued to work away at getting this super car assembled.

Devastating News

As a family, we always ate dinner in our formal dining room. On Sundays, my brother and I had to wear white shirts and a tie. My sisters wore dresses. My grandmother was always present, and she'd have a glass of sherry with each meal. Emma was a truly wonderful person. There was never much conversation. Dinner would be served, we followed the rules of proper manners, and if there were any decrees that needed to be announced, this was where it would happen. Well, during one dinner, my dad totally blindsided me.

He announced that he was leaving Grandview Lumber as Vice President and joining a hardwood kiln business up in Western Michigan. He was going to start commuting there very soon. He would be flying out on Sunday nights and then returning on Friday nights. He added that we should plan on moving there within the next 6 months. Damn! This was more than I could take. Too much information and too much of what I didn't want to hear. Well, he started his commute, flying on Northwestern. Life went on, but I knew that I was faced with having to make some serious decisions. Shoot, I had to go get a Rand-McNally map to find the area that he was talking about. Buckeyes aren't supposed to know much about Wolverine land. It's forbidden!

My dad's mother, 'Susie' Sullivan-McNally, had recently died. It was best to sell off the family business, plus Susie's personal belongings to settle the estate. She had a totally tits '57 Chevy, two doors, soft top, with three on the wheel 283 ci engine, and only 5,000 miles! I wanted that car badly, but as fate would have it, out of my 54 first cousins, and to think that my mother was an only child. Go figure! Catholics reproduce like rabbits. Well, I had a cousin, a real cutie, who was 'knocked up'. In those days, the proper thing to do was to have the child. Her plan was to keep it. Wow, at 17 years old, becoming a mom! Damn. She needed transportation, and the next thing I hear is that her dad, who had married into the family, had taken Susie's car. Bummer! Major bummer! The only drawback was this car was literally titty pink color with a cream color top. If I had gotten that classic, it definitely would have been repainted, probably metallic blue.

To make matters worse, I was told that Myles had sold his metallic blue convertible Chevy to a Golden Bear who was very much on the fringe. Steve was his name, and he and a few other outsiders would randomly show up at John's bunkhouse on the weekends. I never really understood their connection with being allowed to come to the estate, and on top of it, party. Steve, after he got liquored up, would tell us some pretty strange shit. He once got into the fact that he was adopted and that he lived with his older parents alone. He and his friends always wore black leather jackets, pants, vests, and the big Harley kind of boots. They portrayed the same image that the guy in leather in the movie 'The Breakfast Club' manifested. However, these guys never really acted all that tough. They just wanted some sort of small group identity.

We were at a dance up at UA High with our band. For the gig, we had to bring in a different drummer, a guy named Frank, who was a cocky little rich punk. He could sing and he could drum. Our regular singer was out of town, so I went and recruited a singer from another group who, I was told by my girlfriend, 'always needs money'. Randy was a year older than us, but he did have a good reputation as a singer. However, his style was a more traditional, Beach Boys kind of sound, and his range wasn't that strong doing Who and other new sound groups. He could do The Animals, Byrds, McCoys, and The Outsiders well.

Interestingly, none of us out of the three of the band regulars, two hired talents knew the reality of the future. I first would run off with my girlfriend to get married down in the southern states. Kerry, the hired singer, would later hook up with her, get her pregnant and then marry her. They eventually divorced. I believe that she gave up custody of that child back to her ex and moved to California. Then Frank married her, had a couple of kids, but then he OD'd and died, so she ended up a widow. If on that night, we were all jamming together and entertaining the Golden Bear crowd, if someone had told me that we would all have the same connection with the same girl, I would have told them they were crazy, but it happened.

During one of our intermissions, I was out in the parking lots with Gary, the freckle butt, and a few other guys, having a smoke. Steve, the outsider type, who had purchased Myles' totally boss car, came walking by us, then said he had to get home. Steve approached me, asked for a cigarette, then a light, and off he went. I commented to Gary how I thought this was strange because it wasn't all that late, and this guy seemed like a fellow who could do as he pleased. Gary said, "He's probably hooking up with that cute little bitch he has as a girlfriend." That probably was true, because he was usually with this very petite, long-haired, sexy-looking little lady. I think her name was Bonnie. She, like Steve, always wore black leather outfits with a motorcycle kind of jacket. She was petite, long black hair, and sexy eyes.

Well, it was late in the morning the next day. It was a Saturday as I remember, then I got the word from my girlfriend. She told me that Steve had gone home, went into his garage, closed the garage door, started his '57 Chevy, stuck a garden hose in the exhaust pipe and ran it into the passenger part of the car, then put the hose in his mouth. He lit a cigarette that was still burning when the police arrived. He had already called the police before his suicide. Supposedly, he had left a note in the car, but I had never heard what it said. His '57 Chevy went to his girlfriend.

This whole tragic happening left me feeling cold and sad. I was also quite pissed. How could life be so miserable for a 17 or 18-year-old that you would just say 'fuck it' and kill yourself? I think that Steve had polio at one time, because he walked with a pronounced limp, but even that wouldn't be a reason to harm yourself. This was the first real wake-up call for me and the rest of the Golden Bears that nothing was forever. Over the years, we had lost a few, usually to things like leukemia, but these were kids many of us never knew. The gravely ill were in hospitals for months prior to their death, so many were forgotten before they moved on to the happy hunting grounds. Steve's funeral attracted many, but I think most came out of curiosity. The school did nothing to acknowledge the loss or celebrate his life. I can't even remember a tribute in the yearbook. Maybe he was a totally unwanted child from birth until death. Only he and God would know the answer to that.

I still pondered the whole suicide thing. It just didn't make sense, unless maybe a person was terminally ill, and since they didn't have a future, then they decided for themselves as to when they were going to die. In the months that lay ahead, I would end up on a shrink's couch. I became depressed over the breakup with my girlfriend, and I was frustrated about the whole family moving to the frozen tundra of West Michigan. I did, however, get some exciting information from a pool-playing buddy at the ARC one day. He, Tony and I, who were playing 6 ball, were talking about my eventual move to

Michigan. He went to his car, got a map, and came back in and pointed out spots in the Upper Peninsula of Michigan that are great for bear hunting. He had been there on more than one occasion with his father, and I guess they shot some bears. Well hunting, fishing and being outdoors were increasingly becoming a major interest area for me. So, this was exciting and comforting news. Of course, I didn't have a notion about how a person goes about bear hunting, but living on fantasy is what often brings about reality.

I always had a dream of owning an isolated island. This seed was planted, and I was willing to pursue it. One time when I was much younger, and my father had returned from a pickerel fishing trip on Lake Erie, at dinner that night, when he was sharing with us all of the finer details of the trip, he said that he had turned down an offer to buy an island on the lake. All I could think about was how cool! So, I carried that thought with me for many years to come. It was soothing to think that one could have their own little wilderness empire—no neighbors, only the animals of the land, the birds flying over, and all the fishing you could ever want. This sounded to me like a much better option than to head to the suburbs of a town in West Michigan.

The Summer Before Senior Year

The older we got, the crazier everything around us became. Now, as Golden Bears, it was going to be our turn to take over as the internal force running the CRO and ORC gangs. Cool! We had heard that the class prank from the departing seniors and the members of the CROs was placing a VW beetle on top of the high school. Now this school was three stories high, but somehow, they did it. Rumor had it that the car was first dissembled and then re-assembled once it was placed on the roof. We even learned that the car was driven around on the roof. Now that takes either complete stupidity or a lot of balls! It was very 'hush hush' as to who did what. No one wanted the blame, and certainly no one wanted to be arrested for malicious mischief. Well, my dad located a home that he wanted to buy. A five-bedroom colonial in a well-developed neighborhood with many Arlington type amenities. Soon, the family would be moving.

Then one Sunday, out of the clear blue, my dad's older brother, Joseph, and his wife, Lorraine, showed up at our house for cocktails and hors d'oeuvres. My folks were updating them as to their moving plans, and someone remarked how this was going to cause Tommy, as he called me, to miss out on his senior year at UAHS, home of the Golden Bears. Luckily, my uncle and aunt quickly volunteered to have me stay at their house and they would provide transportation for me to and from school. Dang! Only problem was, they lived clear across the river, and down a piece, so any commute was going to take time, but hey, at least I wouldn't have to move to 'Buttphoque Eqypt' and freeze my ass off!

So, now it was just a matter of time before our Arlington house would be sold, and it would become moving day. Sad, very sad, because we had lived in the same house for nearly 20 years, grown up in the neighborhood, and now we were faced with having to venture out into the real world and face realities that maybe we weren't prepared well enough to cope with. Our Arlington ties would become severed, and we'd be challenged with starting all over in places that we were not familiar with, but for now, it would be a day at a time. As Alice Cooper sang, "School's Out Forever." Well, maybe not so, but it was out for the summer. Let it rock!

Water-skiing and riding in a boat was always a luxury for any of us. We had the Scioto River and Griggs Reservoir close by, so a chance to go out on the water was always a treat. Gary, freckle butt, and I met up with Rick and Johnny over at Rick's one morning. Wally, who was our classmate, and a guy who lived near Rick also came over. Johnny knew where his dad hid his ski-boat keys, and he suggested that we all go skiing. The problem was, there were too many of us. The boat was only a 15-footer, and three was enough. You needed a skier, a watcher and a driver. That's all.

Well, we decided using the democrat way of doing things. We drew cards. High cards go, others too bad. My card was an ace, so I was golden, but Gary got a low one. Then a guy named Mike came strolling by. He was a classmate, and he wanted to know what the action was. We told him, and he asked if he could go. So, Rick gave him a card. Rick and Wally both had good cards. Johnny didn't need one; it was his boat. He did say, though, that he'd go with four on the boat. Mike seemed very excited about the prospects of skiing, so I gave him my ace. He was delighted. So, off they went to get the ski boat and spend the afternoon cruising on the reservoir. Gary and I figured we'd go swimming over at the one of the quarry holes.

Gary and I headed over to Donna's house, who lived behind my home. She was there, and she had her mother's convertible. Great! We piled in and took off for Sue's house on the other end of Upper Arlington. We had called her first, so she knew what we hand planned. Both girls were wearing cute little two-piece suits, and Gary and I just had our shorts. Who cares, once you are in the water, you can't really tell who's got what on. Once we got Sue, we headed over to Marble Cliff and plotted our entry into their heavily posted land. We timed it well and headed down one of the dirt roads between runs of the huge limestone trucks. We turned off the radio so that we didn't accidentally detonate any blasting caps on rock busting charges that were already set. We headed to an abandoned portion of the quarry where there was woods and a beautiful green water pond that was about 2 acres in size and probably 15 feet deep.

The water was crystal clear, and you could see lunker bass swimming by all of the time. No matter what the temperature was, these quarry ponds were always very cold yet refreshing. We spent about an hour swimming and goofing around, but then we got out. Gary and Donna grabbed a beach towel, and Sue and I did also. We each went our own way. Sue and I got comfortable up near one of the many sheds and barns that were used for the train's years before. These were the places where we harvested many feral pigeons. We got very close and started making out. I had Sue kinda underneath me as I laid at her side. She told me that she didn't want to have intercourse because someone might come by. I reassured her that no one would show up here.

We continued to make out, and before long, I had her bathing suit top off. In the daylight, her breasts looked very tantalizing with hard nipples and a nice 'A-cup' size. Licking, sucking and feeling her tits was a major turn-on, and soon, she was stroking my hard, hot, and throbbing cock from the outside of my still-wet shorts. She asked me to unzip them and push them down around my knees. I responded in quick order. She then had a hand wrapped firmly around my cock, and she was stroking it ever so slowly. I lowered her bikini bottoms, just enough to expose her pubic hair and her pussy. I slid my hand down to her cunt and three fingers entered her without hesitation. She was wet and very hot. We kept it up for quite a while, and I was waiting to have an orgasm before I was going to light up on the action.

Between finger-fucking her and stroking her clit, I figured that she had about three orgasms. I wanted badly to mount her and slide my hard cock deep into her little pussy, but I knew that she was uncomfortable with this. Plus, she also was rather shy, and even though she had a hot little body, she was pretty modest. She was creaming so well, that I would dip into her pussy, get my fingers good and wet and then rub it on my penis. I would then let her suck my fingers, which she loved to do. After several applications of her very own love juice, she was able to stroke my pecker with little to no friction. It was smooth, hot, and exciting. Within mere minutes, I came like I hadn't in a year, which is a gross exaggeration. She had me so hot, somewhat teased, and terribly aroused that I think I blew two, not one, nut. Whew! What a way to get a suntan!

Donna and Gary were doing much of the same, but what I learned from him later was that they went to the car and screwed there. Donna was less bashful and outgoing than Sue. I remember one boyfriend of Donna's, who told me that once, they were taking the bus home from downtown Columbus and he finger-fucked her all the way home. Sounds a little like Tom Cruise and his hot little hooker in his first hit movie 'Risky Business'.

I hadn't been home long, and I was getting my clothes ready, guitar and trying to get the curl out of my hair. I got a call from Gary. "Hey, you aren't going to believe this. Johnny ran over Mike with the speed boat. I guess it almost cut off his leg."

"Where's Mike now?" I asked.

'He's in surgery' responded Gary. Holy shit, all I could think of was that could have been me. Hell, I was the one who gave Mike the card that got him on the excursion. Damn! Well, in the days and weeks to come, this whole incident was pretty much not discussed. Rumor had it that there were some pretty significant lawsuits being put together and that Johnny was also in trouble with the law and his parents for using a power vehicle without permission. Rick and Wally didn't say much, because they said it was just too sickening to rehash the incident. Later that summer, a chick I knew from St. Andrew's parish, who had gone to the all-girls school, St. Mary's, lost her younger brother in a skiing accident on the same body of water. He had gotten run over by another boat after he had fallen from his skis. Too many of life's ugly realities were surrounding us.

I played that night. We were at the Catholic Information Center at OSU, and the crowd was small, but hey, a booking is a booking. After we finished up, Sue showed, and so, I decided to hitch a ride with her and not travel in the band mobile. I did, however, let them take my equipment, because we would be practicing the next day. Sue was definitely horny from our quarry pond excursion, and we headed to a desolate spot on the river on the Upper Arlington side of the old trestle. We were parked near Route 33, but well off the road on an overgrown path. It didn't take long, but soon, were in the back seat of her beige Comet. The front had bucket sears, so those are pretty useless for making love. In the back, I was able to disrobe her quickly.

There was a full moon, and through the light coming in the back window, it was wonderful staring at her naked body. I kissed her nipples, and I stimulated her vagina with my fingers, and again, she was wet and hot within minutes. I was so excited that I just went ahead and slid my hard cock deep inside her. We were in great harmony with our thrusts. I think that coming earlier in the day made this all the more pleasurable. We stroked for quite a while, and then I came inside of her, and she responded with moans and very deep breaths that she had just come also. I went to pull out of her, but she grasped me hard and asked that I just stay in her. Sue remarked on how great it felt, and it did. We laid there for a while, but for some reason I raised up to look out at the moon, and I could see outline of a police cruiser that was right behind us. I pulled out of Sue and told her, get dressed, like now!

The windows of the car were very fogged up, and sure enough, a cop appeared next to the car with a flashlight. He tapped on the window, and I grabbed what I could to cover myself up. I turned and looked at Sue and said, "No matter what he asks, all we were doing was talking and kissing." Well, naturally, he's got to shine his light in the car, but I refused to open the window very far. He asked what we were doing, and I gave him the pat answer. He then asked for ID. I slid my driver's license, the real one, out the window to him. Sue was still looking for hers. She was able to get dressed and she was sitting behind me. He asked that I get out of the car, so I rolled up the window, got dressed like pronto and exited the car and headed for his cruiser.

Now, the first thing that's going through my head is, that we're not parked in Upper Arlington. This guy is a UA cop. What the hell is he doing cruising the river, looking for parkers? I got in his cruiser and looked at his name badge. Officer Cruise! Seriously? I'm realizing that this guy is a judge, jury, moral counselor and priest. So, the best response was to say very little and admit to nothing. Now the prodding questions. "You two looked totally naked to me." "Were you guys having intercourse?"

"How often are you making love to her?" After a bit and since I hadn't been drinking, he gave up on me and he told me to 'go get the girl'. I went to Sue's car. She was in the front seat, smoking a cigarette, and I told her, "Don't own up to anything. This guy is off his beat, and I don't trust him." Sue reluctantly went to his cruiser and sat in the front seat with this possible weirdo. Sure enough, he tries to play big brother with her. He tells her that she could do much better than me and that she needs to broaden her interests. Then he goes into a story of how he raises toy poodles and that she needs to come to his house to see the puppies. Now he's gone way too far. This guy is looking to score on one of the many young chicks who come to the park to make a little whoopee with their boyfriends. Sue played it cool, started crying, so she couldn't talk, then this bastard writes down his home phone number and gives it to her. She got her license back and headed to the car.

He left, but we sat there for a while, smoking cigarettes and rehashing how we got out of a tight spot. As Susie and I drove away, Sue wadded up his phone number, rolled down the window and tossed it out. Unfortunately for us, this would not be the last time we ran into this creep. It became evident that he literally cruised each and every spot that any parking couples would hang out at. The man had a serious problem.

It was interesting that later that night, as I was rethinking this situation, I remember how my Sociology teach had explained to us how the Second Amendment allows for us to retain weapons to literally protect ourselves from those who in the establishment might try to take us over or exploit us. God help us all if every policeman was as bent as the guy we had to deal with on that moonlit night. For the next few weeks, I continued to share the story as a cautionary note to many of my friends. Gary, Mr. Freckle Butt, my very close friend since 3rd grade, said, "Hell, you should have just beat the shit out of him and gone your merry way." Damn! Gary meant business. He was always a bit volatile, but so was I. I think that he was just learning about my temper and checking to see if I had thought about doing anything to this guy, but I hadn't. I didn't have any ill-will toward him. I just wanted to stay out of his way.

Well, that didn't last long. I was at McKinley Drugs, back in the soda fountain, having breakfast one morning. I was on my way to look at some apartments that some of us were thinking of renting, and a freshly cooked breakfast sounded good. If luck would have it, Officer Poodle Breeder comes in to the diner to get a coffee. Shit! He recognizes me immediately and comes over and makes a remark, "You let that hair get any longer and someone's going to think you're a girl!" My response was quick and simple. "Great, then I won't have to worry about being drafted!" He then just grabbed his coffee and left. I just couldn't shake this guy.

I was headed over to a buddy's house about a week later to do some guitar jamming. As I cruised down a side street, he was clocking traffic and quickly pulled me over. After he went through the traditional pleasantries, like "Do you know why I stopped you?" My response was, "No!" Well, you were going 35 in a clearly posted 25 speed zone. He then directed me to the back of his cruiser. I got in the back seat and knew full well that I would get a ticket. "Well, I can see that you still haven't gotten that haircut. Has anyone ever confused you for a girl?" "No." "Have you ever been confused as one?" "One what?" "A girl?" Just then a car whipped by, he looked at his radar meter, and I didn't see what numbers posted, but he said, 'That's gonna cost you, mister' and off he went. He started chasing this car with me in the back seat. "Hey, let me out. I'm not remaining in this car while you go after some wild-ass speeder!" "Hey, you just shup up and sit quietly back there." So, I did. He finally got the other car to stop, and he got out and went back and told the other driver to follow him. We got back to my car, he ticketed me, and I left. When I went down to pay my fine, which was for going 35 in a 25, I thought most good cops would always give you a 5-mph break. Not this weirdo.

I went in front of the Upper Arlington judge this one evening and admitted that I may have gone faster than the posted speed. He was congenial, but he still fined me. I then asked to make some comments, and the judge gave me the okay. I started to tell the story of how I felt that my life was put in danger by the recklessness of Officer Poodle. An officer, who was in the court, acting kinda like the bailiff, chimed in, "If you have a concern, you take it downstairs and file a complaint!" Ouch! So, I did. Well, if bad luck was gold, I would have been rich.

Again, I was down at McKinley's having a fudge sundae, and who the hell should walk in through the door but Officer Poodle. He gets a coffee to go and walks over to me and says, "You'd better hope that I don't ever catch you out on the street, because you'll be headed to the hospital before going to jail." Damn, this guy thought he was tough. He was threatening me, but who was ever going to believe that? I needed an equalizer! I was 17 years old at the time. I guess that this bully was in his early thirties. I've always been a very emotional person, so if I feel it, I say it, but I thought that it would be better to keep my cool and figure out just how I was going to evade this sucker.

I thought back to a time when the neighborhood bully came over to our house, along with his brother, who was my age. Their target was my brother, who couldn't beat his way out of a paper bag. Richie stopped on a hill that was the border to our property. He started his taunting and name-calling, and my brother and I didn't do much. Richie was too old and too big for us. My mom was home, but at 5 ft. and 100 lbs., she was no help. Plus, if we ran to her, we would be called sissies forever. My brother started to exchange words with Richie, and then he started pushing my brother around, slapping him and threatening him. That was enough!

I ran into the garage, grabbed the first thing that I could find, which turned out to be a ball-peen hammer, and ran up the hill. Just as I reared back to smash

Richie, his brother stepped in my way. Crack! Damn, I hit his younger brother smack in the middle of his forehead. I had never seen so much blood. Man, I had blood all over me. Richie turned kind of a pale gray and grabbed his brother and headed home. They hadn't even rounded the corner to their house and our phone rang. Out came my mom asking, "What the heck did you do to Richie's brother?"

Well, as luck would have it, after all of the threats of lawsuits and counter-lawsuits and the filing of criminal charges, my parents paid for the trip to emergency, stitches, and a new shirt. My dad warned, though, that if Richie continued his provocations, then he'd take care of it. Well, that day came. It was glorious. A bunch of us were out in the street, playing football one evening just after dinner. My brother and sisters were just watching. My buddies and I had a good game going, and there here comes Richie walking down the sidewalk. Damn! As he passed our house, one of my sisters chimed in, "You stay off our yard!" Richie responded by saying, "I'm on the sidewalk, so fuck off!" Then he started in with harassing my brother. He kept it up for some time, and then my dad appeared at the front door, still in his highly starched white shirt. His tie was still on and a dish towel over his shoulder.

As he ran directly across the lawn, right toward Richie, I could see him taking his watch off and his ring on his right hand. Now my dad was one hundred percent 2nd generation Irish. He had a temper like a wildcat, and he was as strong as a bull. He grabbed Richie by the scruff of his neck, literally lifting his fat-ass bully body off the ground, and carried him home that way. Dad was gone for a while, but when he returned, he said as he walked by, "Don't worry about Richie. He won't be around here anymore." Hell, at first, we all looked at each other like maybe he had killed Richie, but then we realized that he had just dropped him off to the care of his parents and then I'm sure that my dad had a 'come to Jesus meeting' with that family.

Well, now I'm in another pickle, and I don't have anyone to turn to except myself. I really didn't have any ill-will toward this poodle-loving cop, but I'd be damned if he was going to threaten me. I thought about making another complaint against him, but I just put that off because cops in those days didn't take kindly to long-haired 'punks'. So, I just went at life a day at a time and waited to see what would happen. God help him, though, if he tried to ever get rough with me. I had totally inherited all of my dad's finer qualities of not having to take shit from anyone, ever!

The 4th of July is always big doings in Upper Arlington. There is a parade, and you just can't imagine how many Golden Bear floats there are. There are also numerous block parties, fireworks, All-Star baseball games, food booths, and many fine doings all over this little suburb. Our band had just finished up a gig at the Ohio State fairgrounds as front runners to Herman's Hermits. I had never signed autographs before, but at this performance, I signed many.

We were so far out of our regular elements that these young, barely pubescent girls thought that we were something cool. Maybe we were, but it just felt awkward. We did look great, suited up in mostly Rolling Stones kinds of attire. This basically meant that you could wear what you wanted to, just don't look like you're headed to the beach. We played for three straight days and got to meet Peter Noone and the rest of the Hermits, which was totally cool. However, we never played any of their songs, and frankly, their songs were happy melodies, but not for parties. I sure wish to this day that I still had my blue flecked Jazzmaster Fender. It was a great guitar.

I think that the 4th came on a Saturday, or at least that's how it seemed. Jon and I, Gary, and others who would come and go started partying on about 2 p.m. Whew, we drank a ton of beer. This kept up for days. On one of the evenings, Jon's parents were gone, and they had left their banana yellow Olds, with white leather interior, and it was a convertible home with keys in it. Off we went. Stroh's in the backseat and us cruising like we owned the world. Cars then, especially like this one, had rocket V-8s in them, and they were faster than hell. The car was huge and very classy. Our favorite song 'Lonely Bull' would be blasting on the 8-track tape player, and we went all over town. We stopped at a few parties, and even hooked up with a couple of cute little hard asses.

However, somehow, when we went parking, one of them referred to a teacher she had the past school year. Jon told me to get out of the car, and let's take a piss. We did. Then he went on to enlighten me that we were with 'jailbait'. He goes, "Ms. So-n-so is a freshman teacher! These girls are 15 at best!" Before you knew it, we were back to where we started, dropping the girls off. Whew! This was frustrating, though, because both were petite, cute, and hot. However, the consequences for doing a minor and the repercussions of cheating on my girlfriend, plus my own conscience just made putting them back on the shelf for a little more aging was the right thing to do. It's like drinking wine before the fermentation process is complete.

I can't remember what night, but one of those connected with the 4th, we were cruising in the super Olds, and we had also picked up Kenny, who was mostly a friend of Jon's and a good guy. We were going down a side street in Arlington and a cat crossed the road up ahead of us. I yelled out, "CAT!" Jon, without missing a beat and turning on the song 'We Got to Get Out of This Place' jumped the curb and off we went, right through the backyards of the homes on the street, chasing this cat in a brand-new, bright yellow, convertible Olds. We didn't get the cat, and we were lucky that we didn't run into any fences either. As a matter of fact, we ended back on the road, and I'm not sure how.

Out came more Stroh's, and we were off. Before the night was over and the sun was cracking the sky to the east, I bet we had chased 4 or 5 more cats. The joke among us was how far and fast can a pussy run. Well, I can tell you, the pussy can outrun and out-dodge a high-priced Olds any day! Later that night, I think it was the 3rd, Jon and I headed over to a neighborhood party in his part of the suburb. It was casual, but very much a high-class party. Guys like David Thomas were there, the neighbor who was on 'Our Miss Books Show', the guy wo owned the local Olds dealership, and many other high rollers.

We ran into Jon's dad, who was just kinda inquiring as to what he had been up to. We gave him some vague answer and then he chimed in, "Frank over there tells me that he could swear that he saw my '88 cruising through his backyard late last night, top down and music blaring. Do you guys know anything about that?" Jon and I looking probably stunned just said, "No!" Then we left. We went back to Jon's house to get his dragster ready for the parade the following day. We stayed in his garage for the remainder of the night, hoping that the cops didn't show because of the cat-chasing deal and getting the '34 super deuce ready to impress the crowds.

On the morning of the 4th, we were up early, possibly because we didn't even sleep the night before. Jon wanted to take the '34 out for a warm-up run, so we pushed it out of the garage, he fired it up, and off we went. Meatloaf would have been proud, because this was one heck of a bat out of hell! Plus, we learned to love the 'meat' when he and Brenda DeCarlo performed 'By the Dashboard Lights'. Now, that's a song we could relate to. Later in life, I was able to see Meat and Patty Russo perform that song, and I think from a fantasy perspective, I fell in love with Patty Russo.

As a matter of fact, I was lucky enough to run into her at 5:00 a.m. in a casino lobby in Mt. Pleasant Michigan, and we actually spent some time together just bullshitting. She was a perfect little angel. I still have her autograph, personalized to me, placed in a special spot in my log lodge in the forest. She's still going strong, and that's totally cool. We had talked about possibly getting together to do some jamming and composing, but you know how things go, life passes us all by, and with that, so do many opportunities. Who knows, Meat had replaced her with some new Patty lookalike. His voice isn't what it used to be and by what I see on the internet, Patty is going strong in the blues/rock arena. Go, girl!

While Jon was out raising decibel hell with the neighborhood, overcame Chris, stepson of the Olds dealer, driving an absolutely tits 442 convertible. Fuck, bucket seats, deep red metallic, matching interior and a Hurst transmission. This baby was set to rock. As Chris and I did a walk around his 'daddy's' car, a cop came cruising by. Thank God it wasn't the dog man. He slowed down, and as we approached his cruiser, he said, "So what's the ruckus about?" We just responded with "Hey, we've got a racing classic that's registered to be in the parade, and it needs a warm-up ride." He was like "That's cool," but he also placed an emphasis on "Let's not break any windows with the noise." Jon was back shortly, and the cop was gone. Whew! Jon jumps out of the '34, with a 312 CID, headers, race cam, slicks, chrome engine parts, and Jon said, "Fuck! I'm overheating!"

Chris and I went and got some rags and the garden hose. I threw some rags over the radiator cap and started to unscrew just as this sucker blew hot radiator fluid and water in my mouth, on my chest, and probably down my front and onto my balls. Ouch! I grabbed that hose and filed myself up with fresh water. I figured that the radiator fluid had to be poison. It may not have been, but the heat from that fluid sure burned the hell out of me. We decided to just let the dragster sit and cool down. It finally cooled, and we went about the process of flushing out the system and filling it back up. Now we were ready for action.

Jon and I cruised down to Kingsdale Center, the origination spot for the parade, and sure enough, we were late. Floats, bands, bikes and all were departing very quickly. We drove right up to the line that was headed out on to Northwest Blvd. A guy kinda stopped us, and Jon gave him a line of BS that was perfect. Before we knew it, we were in the parade line and now part of the action. It was a beautiful, hot, and wonderful day for a parade, and we were set to liven it up. Maybe not to the point of Pluto's float in Animal House, but we could offer some real excitement that many had not seen before. Once in the parade, we would purposely slow way down. As the rest of parade got further in front of us, Jon would rev up the RPM in the 312 CID, three-deuce dragster, and then let her rip. Man, we'd blow smoke, the slicks would squeal, and the car just roared. The crowd went nuts! We were able to get this done about 20 times before the dragster started to smoke and overheat. We made it past Lane Avenue into old Arlington, and there, we had to pull off on a side street and let the car cool down. I would wager to this very day, I'd bet that people are still talking about the super deuce dragster, with no club or association affiliation, which stole the show at the UA annual 4th of July parade.

Chris picked us up in the 442 convertible, and we just let the dragster sit and cool down. Jon was fearful that the block may crack and that would be devastating to such a classic car. For the rest of the day, we just hit parties and went to food booths. We were hitting the Stroh's pretty hard, but hey, it was a holiday. We eventually hooked back up with Kenny, and we all just cruised for much of the day. There were hydroplane races, including Miss Budweiser, down at Griggs on the river, so we headed there. Talk about loud! Shit, Jon's coup couldn't compare to the noise produced by these super boats. Lo and behold, we were down there, hanging together and drinking Stroh's. Here comes one of the jailbaits, or so we thought—girls from a few nights before. She starts hanging on me and I thought, hey, what the heck, she'll be 16 sooner or later. Well, she told me that she was 18 and that she had been held back in school. This sounded plausible.

She and I ventured up to a high point of elevation in the park, where there were few, if any, spectators. She had a beach blanket with her, and instead of sitting on it, she put it over us. Quickly, we were engaged in a lip lock, and she was grabbing at my pecker like a baby robin going after a night crawler. I had on jean cut-offs, and she had on short shorts with a skimpy halter top. Small boobs and a great butt. She was going after me like a starving child in Africa who hadn't eaten in a week. What I didn't clue in on was that she had been drinking, either the night before, this day, or both. She had the various beer can tabs around her fingers. When she grabbed onto my very erect, ready to go, hugely enlarged pecker, she just about did a Bobbit on me. Damn, those beer tabs were like razors. She was wanting to jack me off with metal in her hands.

This girl just couldn't be what she portrayed herself to be. I cut off the action, headed back to my buddies, and told them, "We've got to drop her off."

Thankfully, my dick healed, and all was well. I didn't want to be like R. P. McMurphy and have to explain to some prison shrink that "Hey, you get that close up to the beaver, you don't ask for a driver's license…" I wanted to be more or less in line with the rules of play as society dictates them. We headed back to Jon's, took a dip in the pool, and started to gear up for an evening of fun, fireworks, partying and girls. My lady was off visiting friends and family out of town, so I more or less had a carte blanche to act as an asshole.

My family wasn't all that much into 4th of July fireworks, but they did always barbeque a big meal. We did cruise by there, picked up some grilled lobster, ribs, chicken and sides, then went on our merry way. Chris continued to have the 442, so we figured that was our ride of the night. We had heard of a big party down at Penny's house on the country club grounds, so we were planning on heading there. We cleaned up, brushed our teeth, put on some clean madras shirts and khaki shorts and sandals, then headed out. This would be a place that we'd want to be. It was next door to the Galbreath mansion, and I do mean mansion.

Shit, they had a bowling alley down their basement. I had gone to school with the two girls, but I never had much contact with their older brother. They were all cool. I always wanted to make a move on Mimi, but I just never got up the courage. She was cute, thin, and just a very nice person. Her older sister Judy was very much the same, but they lived in a far different world than I. When you have John Kenneth Galbreath as your grandfather, life just naturally aligns much differently than it does for the rest of us plebs. As we headed out of Jon's neighborhood in Chris's 442, I'm not sure who said, "Let's see what this baby can do," but I want to tell you we went from 25 to God-only-knows-how-fast within seconds.

The sad thing was, as we rounded this corner, a lady was getting out of her car on the driver's side. Chris was at warp speed. She had to slam her car door and press her body up against the side of her car as he tried to negotiate cars on both sides of this narrow road. Kenny and I, who were in the back seat, hit the floor, fearing that Chris was going to crash. He didn't, but as we looked back, the lady was on the ground, and we were headed out of there at a huge speed. It took a couple of days, but Chris was hunted down by the UA police detectives. They wanted to charge him with reckless driving and endangerment. Shit! Well, only time would tell if he was able to cruise through that legal maze.

We did end up at Penny's, and there was a party going on, but it was more girls than guys. The word I got was that Hillary, a neighbor to Penny, who was in the same class as me, hence a Golden Bear, was hot on me. This caught me by surprise, because it was as though once one of these debutants liked you, it was your responsibility to like them. Well, I just wasn't subscribing to that notion. I'd heard that Hillary and a bunch of other gals were out on the golf course running through the greens sprinkling system. It sounded fun and something that I shouldn't miss, but Gary, the Pollack, who was my fishing buddy and friend, showed up and advised me to just stay clear.

"There's plenty of fine pussy around, and Hillary is too high maintenance for you." So, I moved on from that possible encounter. What I had soon learned, so many of the notes and letters that I had written to my girl Mary, who moved to Phoenix with her reportedly dike mom, were circulating among these Golden Bear debutants. They had gotten them through Mr. Freckle Butt, who had taken them from my house, paybacks for leaving him naked at the river! Shit, these girls thought that I was some sort of new version of Johnny Wad. They didn't know if they wanted a piece or if I was just a gold digger pecking my way into their pants. I never hooked up with Hillary. She was way too pristine for me. She was a nice little lady, but not a person who I could see myself with. So on to greener pastures. Interestingly, but not surprising, in our senior year, Hillary was crowned Homecoming Queen. This was an honor that she definitely deserved.

Gary and I were hanging in the lower level of the Thirsty I one evening, hoping to score on some north end chicks. I can't remember where my girlfriend was, but this was only a one-night fling. There weren't many people around, so we just hung out and drank some Stroh's. Gary went out into the hallway to make a phone call, and when he came back in, he goes, "You won't believe who is in here." I just stared at the door, hoping that it was Suzanne Somers or someone of renown. Well, here enters a tall, very cute chick, with bite-sized tits and a beautiful complexion. Damn, she was pretty. She looks around, Gary says "Hi," and she moves on without even acknowledging his existence. He looks at me and says, "That's Kristina from grade school." I responded, "Bullshit." She could have trodden water in a garden hose, but as I gazed at her flawless complexion, shapely body and wonderful beauty, it *was* her. Lesson learned is, why hassle the ones who just haven't come into their own while they are young? Look at their moms, was what my dad would always say. It made sense. Kristina's mom was a knockout. She was at the school as a homeroom mom and many other things all of the time. She was classy, tall, flawless, and sexy. Well, so was her offspring.

Helen and Ann were two other girls that we had grown up with, but they had gone to St. Mary's High School. I ran into Helen at a party at Gary's apartment two years after we had graduated. She had turned 'hippie', no bra, braided hair, flowery clothes, and a body to die for. Again, here was a girl who was as plain as a nun, who blossomed into a fabulous looker, and I couldn't get off base one with her. She and the rest of the gang were headed to some sort of mega concert out east. I had never heard of the town Woodstock, New York, and since I was never into drugs, I decided that their planning was too loose, and the scene was not for me. Ann was a girl who I grew up with and I always treated her with respect, but she was very plain, and she didn't exude much sex appeal. However, when I ran into her and Kathy at an early reunion, damn she looked nice. Kathy also was looking great, and we even danced. She shared with me that she had recently gotten divorced, and she might as well have been rolling out a red carpet from her to me so that I could hook up with her. That would have been cool, because I had always held a certain degree of sexually wanting her. It certainly didn't happen.

Our band was having quite a few gigs this summer, and it was getting harder to keep everything in balance. We had the good fortune of playing warm-up to Tommy James and the Shondels at a huge frat party. Our singer got busted for drinking by the campus police because he was the youngest one there. This gigantic street dance ended by midnight, because the cops made it end. Fine with us. We were already paid and packing to hit the road. I packed intoxicated Greg, our singer, into the back of my car, and then we covered him with guitar cases, mic stands, and a whole bunch of band paraphernalia. I was planning on taking him and John, our drummer, home, because they both lived on the north side, and I was headed to pick up Susie before I went home. Well as luck would have it, Greg, who warned me that he didn't feel well, puked all over the backseat of my mom's car. Fuck! John, who was usually calm, cool and collected, said, "There's a carwash up ahead, pull in there!" I kinda hesitated, because this was the 'short north' part of Columbus, and you needed to be one tough hombre to hang out there, but then again, I thought I got John with me, who was tougher than shit. His older brother Frank had a reputation that transcended Columbus for toughness. So, into the self-wash we went.

John and I unpacked the car, pulled out Greg, sat him in a corner, and went to work on the car. It didn't take long, and the car was totally spiffy, smelled fresh, like coconuts, and we were able to repack and go our merry way. Plus, no one came by to hassle us. There sure was a lot of drag racing going on. High Street was filled with all kinds of supercharged 409s, 327s, 396s, 283s, 389s, and many more high-performance engine configurations. You could hear the squealing tires for miles. I got John home and then Greg. I more or less just let Greg to his front door, which was locked. I leaned him against it and then rang the doorbell. Then, off I went, like the Road Runner scurrying away from a lit bomb. I heard about it the next day, though. Greg called me and said that his parents told him that they wanted him to stay away from me. I was a bad influence! What the fuck! That young punk was the one who went hog wild on the free beer at the frat party. He was the one who guzzled one right after another so that no one knew exactly how much he had drunk. Shit, my response was to kick his ass, because I'm sure that chicken-ass blamed everything on me.

I finally got to Susie's at about 1:00 a.m. I waited outsider of her parents' home for a few minutes, and sure enough, she appeared from around the back of the house. She hopped in the car and off we went. "I hope that everyone was asleep." She responded, "They were!" We headed to an area of new homes in the far north region of Upper Arlington. I found a nice, secluded cul-de-sac street that we drove halfway around, and we parked. We made out for a bit, but then we started talking. She was having feelings like I was. This relationship was going far past puppy love or just infatuation. In reality, we were falling in love, fast!

Love is a strange emotion, because it affects you more emotionally than any other way. I always felt very excited and happy when I saw Sue. We always had nice times together, and we shared in my interests. We were physically attracted to each other, and we had common goals and dreams. We even talked some about having children. This was pretty heavy stuff for a couple of teenagers to be going over, but hey, we were in love, and there's no biological clock that controls when that may or may not happen. We also both knew that if we became exclusive to each other, this would eventually cut us off from many of our friends. It would basically limit us to hanging out with other couples who were closely bonded and in love. I gazed into Susie's eyes as we talked, and there were tears streaming down her face. I asked her if something was wrong, and she just said, "I'm just so very happy."

A flash of headlights came across my car, and another vehicle entered the cul-de-sac. As it approached, you could see by the streetlights that it was a cop. Sure enough, it was, and Sue and I were just sitting there, smoking cigarettes. Damn, when the cop opened his door, I could see that it was the poodle king! Fuck! He approached the car with a flashlight and shined it in on us. "Hey kids, isn't it a bit late out for you to be parking? Hey, it's you two, I want to see some ID!" he exclaimed. So, we both gave him our driver's licenses and he just stood there and shined his light on them. "I thought I told you that I didn't want to see you both again." he quipped.

"Officer, we're just here enjoying the warm night and talking," I stated.

"Hey, if I wanted anything from you, I'd ask," he responded. "Listen, you kids can't be parking all over hells half-acre. There are creeps out here that prey upon folks like you. Now, pack it up and go home. Next time I'm going to cite you for a curfew violation," then he left. Sue and I both realized that he was keeping his distance because we had our clothes on. We were actually in Upper Arlington, and there was a chance that other cars could come by. He certainly didn't want to mess with me with Sue there as a witness. His curfew line was pure bullshit, because there was only a curfew for 17-year-olds and younger in Columbus and not in Arlington.

Sue and I remained there for quite a while, and as luck would have it, that pervert drove by again about an hour later. He flashed us with his spotlight, he could tell we were just sitting in the car, and off he went. This guy was becoming desperate for the flash of a little flesh. He'd have to go home and play with his puppies, because he wasn't going to get his jollies off of our action. Our action was purely intellectual and emotional that night.

The days of summer were rolling by way too fast. There was much to do, but there was also a ton to think about. The Vietnam War was escalating, and many of our older friends were getting drafted to go overseas to this little country that France had once occupied, and fight 'someone'. We never really learned who the enemy was in this war. It was one of those 'north vs. south' things, but that doesn't tell you much when everyone speaks the same language and they all look alike.

CRO and ORC orientation for the junior class was coming up and so were the football tryouts. Again, the football coach advised me to just stay home. He too must have had a thing about long hair. I warned him, though, because the word was out that the Golden Bears would be playing the Eagles of Watterson. He'd better be prepared for the worst. Marv just scoffed at me and then laughed. The 'Little Sisters of Charity couldn't beat anyone'. It was evident that he hadn't done his scouting homework the year before, and he was way too confident in what the Golden Bears were capable of. Shoot, the Eagles had 4 or 5 OSU draft prospects. UA had none. I wouldn't be playing, so I guess that I just accepted the fact that I'd be a spectator and leave it at that.

Bryan, my Watterson buddy, and I would finish out much of August fishing ponds that were owned by OSU and very off limits to anyone unless you had Woody Hayes connections. Well, Bryan was a top prospect for OSU, and he got us permission to fish in these gated waters. Damn, did we catch lunkers. It was 5-pounder after 5-pounder. Every so often, we'd get a 6 or a 7-pounder. Heck, the bull frogs around these ponds probably weighed in at 2 pounds each. This was a fun experience, and doing outdoor things for the immediate years to come was something that Bryan and I did frequently.

Here Comes the Fall

My parents and sisters were preparing to move to West Michigan. The house on Andover sold immediately, and that was a sad day for all of us. After all of those years living in a house that my dad had designed and had built, it was tough to walk away from. I was slowly moving stuff to my aunt and uncle's home up in Hillards. I got a very private bedroom along with a full bathroom, so I was pretty well set as far as privacy went.

I could tell, though, that they weren't accustomed to a guy like me, who was always on the go, who had a serious girlfriend, played in a band, shot pool a lot, stayed out to all hours of the night, and traveled around to places like Cedar Point, Buckeye Lake and other points of interest and fun. They were very conservative, and at times, very unrealistic as to what your typical Golden Bear, aka CRO '67, was allowed to do. What I soon discovered was that the best approach with them was just to give them pat answers to all of their questions and always tell them what they wanted to hear. If I was going out for extended periods of time on the weekend, then I would arrange to stay at a friend's house. The good news was, I still had thirty days before all of these moves were final.

Susie and I continued to talk a lot about the notion of staying together and getting married. I'm not sure how we ever finally arrived at this decision, but after going and looking at apartments, checking on jobs, exploring night school options, we started talking about getting married. School started, and I wish I could say without incident, but I didn't make it through enrollment without a major confrontation from the Assistant Principal, Dave. He came over to me immediately for long hair. After a brief shouting match, he escorted me to the door and told me not to return unless my hair was cut. Well, what perfect timing.

My mom had been telling me to get my senior pictures taken, so it was time to see the barber. Within days, I looked like a new man. Shorter hair, and my senior pictures were completed. Now I could return to school, get enrolled, and start the year off right. However, the clash over the hair, my parents moving, not being involved in sports, the reality of the Vietnam War, my love for Sue, the eventual end of the band, and so much other shit was influencing me to take charge of my life and go after what I really wanted. That was a life with my 5 ft. tall, 95 lb. little brunette whom I loved so dearly.

Heck, if I was married and we had our own place, then fuck the perverted poodle cop. We would be making love at our own place and not sneaking around, trying to find a place of privacy and seclusion. Sue and I continued our heart-to-heart talks, and at school, I researched marriage laws for surrounding states. I found that in South Carolina, 17 and 16-year-olds could get married after a 'so many day' wait. So, our plan moved into action.

We decided to take my mom's car, and I would use gasoline charge receipts to purchase gas. I had a fairly large amount of money saved up from playing in the band, so that would pay for our expenses. We wanted to get a jumpstart on our parents finding out until we had left the state, so we planned our elopement for a Friday night. I talked with the bass player from our band, Jim. I told him everything that we were going to do, and he thought it was cool. I asked him to call my parents and Sue's parents at midnight after the football game. He agreed. We were going to depart right after school, so we'd be well down into Kentucky by the time anyone even knew that we were gone.

At first, there may have been some hesitation, but once we hit the road, it became an adventure. Sue and I were very happy together and enjoyed every mile of our long trip. After crossing the Ohio River and heading into Kentucky, I believe that we checked into a motel in Pikesville. Being together and sharing the same place, bed, and moment in time was exhilarating. We made love most of the night and then ventured out for breakfast as we resumed our trip. Each place we stopped at for lodging, food, bathroom, breaks or gas became special. We collected mementos from each little port as we traveled. We even sang songs together, because the radio reception in the mountains totally sucked. We had to head to the county seat of each state we were in to check on getting married. All the southern folks that we dealt with were warm and courteous.

We weren't getting any good news. We kept getting sent further south as we were turned down by the first few states because of Susie's age. We knew if we lied, then her father for sure, being a former FBI agent and lawyer, would have annulled in a heartbeat, and it wouldn't be because of me, but because we didn't think that he was ready to lose his daughter. So, we continued our journey. In South Carolina, we were directed by one of the judges to go get blood tests at the local hospital, which we did. Then there was a three-day waiting period to get the license. Well, after the rests and the wait, we were up at his residence, when somehow, it came out that we needed written permission from her parents for her to get married. Holy shit; that wasn't going to happen. The only way around it was if she was pregnant. She wasn't. Well, it appeared that the best of a well-planned scheme often failed. This one was crashing fast. We had two options—stay in the south and take up shop and live there until whenever or start heading north and enjoy the long journey home, because once we got there, our freedom just may be restricted a bit. Well, we elected the latter.

We even decided to each call home and tell our folks that we were alright and that we'd be coming home within a few days. My parents were fine about it. My mom just basically told me to drive safely and take my time getting home. Susie's dad was a little more controlling. He initially threatened to have the police pick me up for taking his daughter out of the state without her parents' permission. Oh well, he was a dad and dads have to have control over things. He eventually just hung up on Susie, but she wasn't concerned because she always said that he has a hard time expressing his emotions. Well, we traveled for about 2 more days, staying in a nice motel every night. The loving continued, and the sweet smell of this gorgeous little lady still resonates in my mind. She was definitely a keeper, but who knew what the future would hold for us. Together, we were one and united; apart, the pressures of family, society, and economic issues would eventually be the death of our relationship. Also, the illusion of love is best left to Romeo and Juliet.

When we arrived back in Golden Bear land, I just dropped Sue off at home and then headed to my place on Andover Road. It was evening, about 8:00 p.m. My parents were in the living room, drinking hi-balls, and both were courteous and kind as I entered the house. They asked about the trip. They wondered if we were married and otherwise there wasn't much to discuss. However, my mom said that there was some juvenile detective who I had to see in the morning. Great! Well, I guess that Susie's dad had filed some sort of Man Act complaint against me, so as a courtesy to him, they were going to put the fear of the Lord in me. I arrived and got one of these 'I'd throw ya in jail if I thought it would do any good' kinda cops. I was not impressed. The older and wiser I got, the more I could see the personality flaws in many of these punks. So many of them had a little too much David Toma in them. I know David fairly well. This style of being a so-called tough guy on the side of the law means nothing to me.

If you want answers, ask me. If you want honestly, trust me. If you want a citizen who supports you, don't attempt to exploit my girlfriend with your manipulative tactics. It doesn't fly. As luck would have it as I'm sitting there getting this prepaid lecture from this polyester king pin, Officer Poodle walks by. Damn! He looked, stopped, and poked his head into the room. "Hey Sarge, can I inject a comment here?" "Sure," belted out the Sergeant between coffee burps. "I've had nothing but trouble from this punk. He used to have long hair; he's a troublemaker." Then the ass left. I looked straight at the cop and said, "Tell me what record you have on me, or what trouble this guy is suggesting that I've caused. I've got complaints on file as to his reckless police practices, and I'll gladly review those with you. I also have other major concerns as to his lack of readiness or mental fitness to be a UA cop that I'll talk with you about also." I smiled and sat back down. He folded and advised me that he didn't want to see me down there again. My response was, "Why should you? In all these years, you've never seen me before and I doubt if you'll see me again." Hasta la vista, Mr. Detective.

Susie's dad was all business about this getting married thing, and he immediately put her to work. I think that he wanted to prove that life was not all that it was cracked up to be, so having her work just may want Susie to run back to your comfort zone of allowances, use of the car, staying out late and other things that seniors do that aren't so 'out there'. Susie stood strong—she went to work, continued with school, and we saw each other on the weekends. When I had band gigs, it was hard, because her time out of the house was being monitored. However, I was not Clyde, and Susie wasn't Bonnie! He did like to play the guitar, and many times, when I showed up to visit or pick up Sue, I would show him a thing or two on the acoustic 6-string. He enjoyed that. He was still very reluctant to have me take Sue out of the house, because I think that he worried that we might never return. Possibly!

My parents moved, and I was off to my uncle's. It was obvious that my life was in a huge transition. I could only manage so many things at once. As time passed, Sue was wearing down from the grueling schedule of both school and work. Sue and I were seeing less of each other. We'd talk on the phone, but it was usually late at night, and her parents in particular would bitch about her tying up the line at bedtime. Their well-thought-out plan was working. They would bombard her with questions about college, living arrangements, food, cars, clothes, travel vacations, children, and the whole gambit of marriage, and it was taking its toll. She was succumbing to the attraction of being a regular carefree teen for at least one more year. I could sense it, and I needed to confront it. I had a huge emotional investment in this little lady, and I could envision a future with her, but I needed her to be on the same page as me.

Fall was upon us, and the chill and frost of the morning signaled that we were getting close to the end of the football season. Now, the clash of the Titans was a certainty. The Golden Bears of Upper Arlington, the conference champions, were going to take on the undefeated Eagles of Watterson High School. The hype was huge. The press and everyone downplayed the explosive power of Watterson under the expert coaching of Dick Walker. Most felt that this game would be just another feather in the cap of Coach Marv for the Golden Bears. Plus, they were playing on Golden Bear turf.

Well, the CROs and the ORCs knew how to do it up well with a bonfire and a beer bust before the game. The only problem was, we were way out at Twin Lakes, up in the Dublin area off of Route 33, having our social cocktail hour. It was a bit far to be able to reach the game for kickoff. Everybody guzzled and drank like there was no tomorrow, and soon, it was time to depart as a caravan. Sue and I were some of those who were the last in and the last to leave. We followed Rick and Rickie out onto the windy river road, and sure enough, Rick M. went way too far left, crossed the center line, and hit head-on with a north-bound car. Shit! I asked Sue to just sit in the car and went up to the wreck and looked inside Rick's mother's new Thunderbird. What a fucking mess. Rick, the passenger and my water-skiing buddy, basically had the front of his face ripped off. His nose was literally resting on his forehead, and his head was hanging back, as if his neck was broken. Rick the driver had numerous cuts and injuries. It was a gruesome sight. Neither could talk and we didn't even know if they were alive. The driver of the other was okay, and he was very concerned about who he had hit.

Sue and I headed to the nearest phone and called the police and an ambulance. They arrived very quickly, and we headed off to the game. Well, for the Golden Bears, that wreck was just about as gruesome as their awful play during this match of champions. Again, it was as though the Golden Bear coaching staff had missed the responsibility of scouting the power and diversity of talent on the Watterson team. Watterson jumped their ass and walked away with a 32-0 score. This cast Watterson into the limelight of being one of the greatest football teams ever assembled to play on Ohio soil. The great ego and narcissism of the Golden Bears had been deflated. For many, this was the ultimate let-down of their four years of being a Golden Bear. The Golden Bears were again taking a lesson in the fact that life can suck. Reality bites, and you need to get ready, because the party is just about over! The Golden Bears were not Titans, they were 'so-so' at best. A bunch of great guys in a super suburb needing to embrace their limits.

For weeks to come, we checked on Rick M. and Rick B. at the hospital. Both came through the collision miraculously. Rick B. was going to need a lot of plastic surgery. He had several hundred stiches in his face, and his nose had to be reattached. Rick M. was much luckier. He had many stiches and contusions, but he got out of the hospital far before Rick B. did. When Rick B. got home from the hospital, he had a brand-new cherry red, high-performance 289 CID Ford Mustang waiting for him in the driveway. I thought, *what a contradiction*. Holy crap, he had just barely survived a drinking and driving head-on collision, and yes, we were all grateful that he was alive. A new hell-raising car!

Rick's family was like that. They had adopted kids, with Rick being the youngest. His older sister had her many run-ins with trouble, but as Rick would explain, his parents always bailed her out. Rick, who started to become a closer friend, seemed to have some real problems with being adopted and with the numerous scars he had. I would stop by to visit him quite frequently, and he would just fly into these fits of rage for no apparent reason. It was like him to try and pick a fight. Several times, I almost obliged him, but then I thought that I didn't have any issues that would make me mad at him. So, I would usually just bear hug him until he calmed down.

One time, though, Jon, Wally, and I were over at Rick's, and he got this crazy idea that we should box. Wally was a good boxer, but he wasn't too interested because he wore thick glasses, and he didn't want to take them off. Besides, we were all dressed and groomed to go out, and no one really wanted to get sweaty. Rick kept pushing and then the other two chimed in, so on went the gloves, and I got the short straw to box with Rick. He had some speed, but he certainly didn't have the punch, so I plummeted him without embarrassing or hurting him. I just wanted to let him know who was in charge. He hugged me as it was obvious he was clearly out gunned and then said, "Before I enlist in the Marines, I'm going to take on Tony…" "What? Are you nuts? He'll beat you to a pulp!" I exclaimed. "I just want to know what real pain feels like and I want to see how well I can do against him," was Rick's response. Well, lucky for Rick, no one rumored that statement. Anyways, I doubt if Tony would even pay any attention to a passive threat or challenge from Rick. Tony could have beaten him over the phone. I think that each one of us had major concerns about Rick's volatility and his need to act out. He was a wonderful guy who would do anything for you, but emotionally, from the time of the wreck on, he was in a process of deterioration.

As the holiday season approached, it was becoming more apparent that Susie and I were having some issues. Exactly what they were, I wasn't sure. I could sense that things were not the same. I was working as the lead man to find Jon, Gary my fishing buddy, and I an apartment. We wanted a home base near OSU for partying and for crashing. Gary, Mr. Freckle Butt, wanted in on the action, too, but his commitment to us was kinda shaky. Sue picked me up at the ARC where I was playing pool on a rainy Friday afternoon. She was going to take me to my uncle's place, but I had scored on renting an apartment on 11th Avenue, and I wanted her to see it. The only way to enter this dump was from the back, up the wooden stairs, and in the back-kitchen door. We didn't have much furniture yet, but at least it was clean, had three bedrooms, one bath, a kitchen and a front room. For $50.00 per month, it was a deal.

The only problem was the neighborhood. This was a white trash area, and crime was a way of life for many who lived there. Susie and I looked around as I turned on the stereo. I played the Rolling Stone's latest 'Let's Spend the Night Together', and before you knew it, we were arm in arm on the one bed in the place. We got it on, but as I undressed Sue and massaged her clit and sucked her nipples, she just wasn't responding with the same passion that she usually had. As I entered her, she made a comment about me not cumming in her. I heated up, and we went from her being under me, to her being on top of me, eventually I came inside her, like I always did. When we separated and started getting dressed, she was brushing her hair and she looked down at the bed and on the covers was a large wet spot. She hit it with her brush and screamed out, "I told you that I didn't want you cumming in me!" I just said,

"Hey, I thought that I pulled out in time!" That didn't fly, and we had a long, silent ride home, all the way to my uncle's on that cold, rainy afternoon.

When she dropped me off, she was very vague as to what she was doing for the weekend and absolutely not the least bit cheery. I played with the band that Saturday and headed home afterwards. No Susie, no Debbie, nobody. Something was way wrong. I talked with Sue on Sunday night. I remember being in my studio bedroom, propped back in a chair, staring at the best Playboy pin-up on all time, Donna Michelle. The most gorgeous, natural beauty on earth! Eventually, Pattie McGuire would hold a close second, but Donna was again the sexiest of all time. Well, I was talking with Susie and so I thought hey, it's time to lay it on the line. What's up? Sue became honest and made a comment to the effect that she thought that we just ought to resume our normal lives, put the marriage stuff on hold, and maybe even see other people.

I was devastated. Holy shit, we were going from having everything together emotionally and physically. We just had to now face the realities of hard work and true companionship to make it work. Sue shared with me that I needed to listen to the song by the Monkees 'I Want to be Free' and then I would understand. I tuned into WCOL that night and waited for this song to play. I had one of my many guitars ready so that I could learn the tune quickly. The song was full of metaphors of being free like the waves out on the blue sea. It talked about being close to her, guiding her, but letting her do her own damn thing. No way! She was bailing out and trying to add a little romance to it. Bullshit!

In the days and weeks to come, it was very apparent that we were in major decline as lovers. We shared lockers next to each other, so it was tough having to face her 3 to 4 times per day. Then to top it all off, I hear that Gary S., the guitar-playing dude who thought that he was so tough, and whom I whipped like a cup of cream in PE wrestling, liked her. What added insult to injury was when I learned from my lady friend and confidant Cindy, was that he and Sue used to go out a lot. I called Sue on it, and she admitted that it was like a physical thing, that she would be attracted to Gary. I guess that she liked broad shouldered, long-haired, guitar playing dudes. I had no ill-will toward Gary; however, I had lost a huge amount of respect for Sue.

In those days, life was rather upside down. Guys could screw around, chase other chicks, and still expect their steady gal to be there for them. If a girl did this, she was a slut. Sue and I became distant friends, at best. It really depressed me, and after talking with my family doctor, he referred me to a local shrink. The few times that I went to see him, I was rather scared by some of the patients who were in his waiting room. I mean coocoo; these folks were nuts! He and I had some meaningful discussions, and he basically advised me that I was trying to move through life too fast. I was already going after dessert way before I had sampled dinner. Made sense, but it still didn't take the hurt away. Then, one weekend, I heard this: his son had attempted suicide. I never really followed up to see if he killed himself or not. I had heard that he hung himself in their garage. It was time to either quit seeing the shrink or get someone else. I quit.

It wasn't long before we were in our second semester at school—the homestretch for all of us Golden Bears. Unfortunately, much was coming apart at the seams. Rick and Rickie both had been reassigned to junior class. They had missed too much school because of their injuries. Plus, neither one of them were ace students to begin with. Many of the long-standing couples, including Sue and I, had broken up. So much of what looked perfect was not.

The Vietnam War was really bearing down on all of us guys, because not only was the war escalating, but the draft ratios were increasing. Again, so many of the guys a year or two older than us were coming back crippled or dead. The list published in the newspapers would make you sick. Guys who I knew as tough hombres were dead. Their families were devastated, and none of us fully understood who or what the hell we are fighting for. I got my class ranking form one day, and out of about 625 students in the senior class, I was about 601. Fuck!

However, I couldn't give a shit about school. It was meaningless bullshit, and all of us needed to be more concerned and educated about what the hell was going on in the world. I got into a pattern of stopping at school, then splitting with my buddies Gary, Mr. Freckles, and sometimes a few others. We'd head over to Rick M's house for breakfast. He would make the best eggs that you could imagine. Lightly whipped eggs, sour cream, bacon bits, green peppers, and whole wheat toast. Damn, that was good! Rick, whose mom was divorced from his father, lived well. He had decided that since he had been flunked capriciously that he would just stay home for the remainder of the year and show up in the fall. He was a remarkably good-looking guy, and he went about life like he had no worries.

One day, he and Gary took off to go attend to some business, and they left me at Rick's house to 'guard the fort'. Rick was like Ferris Bueller, so I knew that they'd be back soon; however, they weren't. I had to meet a guy down on the OSU campus to put together a gig contract for the band, so my only transportation was Rick's Honda. I had ridden a lot, and taking his machine didn't seem like any big deal. So, I went out, checked the gas, and it appeared that all was well. I started that puppy up and zoom, I was out of there. I was cruising through the neighborhood of my coach, Hillary the beauty queen, the Galbreaths, Phillips, and many of the other notables who surrounded Scioto Country Club. I was coming down a curvy street when a burgundy, convertible Cadillac came from the opposite direction, right down the middle of the road. It was a lady driver, who probably had one too many martinis, and she clipped me hard. I flew through the air to the sidewalk, and the bike skidded down the road.

Shit! I was definitely hurt, and the convertible was gone. Luckily, a neighbor who had heard the screech called an ambulance, and off I went to Riverside Hospital. Once at the hospital, I was assigned to a room where a lady doctor was assigned to take care of me. She came in, and after a very careful examination, she stated that I had a lot of debris impaled into my skin, but no broken bones or internal injuries. She left but later returned with a surgical pan, many tools, and an assistant. They flipped me over, she uncovered my butt, and then she went to work on extracting stones and whatever from my ass. The doctor talked a lot as she moved from foreign object to foreign object.

It was funny when she said, "Hey, you're lucky that you're not the guy in the next cubical. He was skateboarding on Mirror Hill, down on the campus, and he ran into a parked car. He has both arms and legs broken." After a few hours, she had all of the cinders and other crap removed from my butt, arms, and hand. She carefully wrapped everything in gauze, and then I was good to go. I kinda looked like Boris Karloff in The Mummy, but I felt better. I learned later from Rick that his bike was okay, and he was more worried about how I was.

Eventually, I was pretty much healed and able to get down to the UA Police Department and file a complaint about the reckless driver. As luck would have it, I ran into Detective 'I-know-it-all-and-I'm-gonna-throw-you-in-jail' to the queen of poodles, who never knew me, but he felt that my girlfriend could do better. I filed my complaint, but I'm sure that it ended up in a waste basket sooner after I left the building. These creeps would have rather been confirming my fatality than searching for who may have run me over. Hey, shit happens, and one has to learn to roll with the punches in order to get by in this world.

The apartment thing started to become a place to gather. We had some competition, because Johnny, Bone, Wally, Grady, and a few others including Rick, and Mr. 289 had gotten their own place. One night, late, Gary, Jon, and I were headed up to our apartment, and Johnny and Boner showed up to party. We got to the top of the fire escape, and Gary made a comment to Johnny that they weren't going to be partying that night. It was too late. Plus, we had let some of them into our place with a hidden key and a bunch of mule deer steaks were missing; so was some beer. Johnny had a six pack in his hand, and he slammed it down on the floor of the fire escape. Naturally, all the bottles broke, and I think that Jon chimed in, "What a waste."

Well, Johnny started provoking a fight with Gary. Big mistake. I'd had a fight with Gary in the past, and he was far too tough to mess with. He was big, strong, and pretty fearless. Johnny had to prove his point and not back down. John's best offense was reciting all of the tough guys who would have come over to kick your ass. That didn't fly with Gary. He was too close to Tony and so many others, plus he was tougher than shit himself. He just invited John and company to leave. They did. Thankfully! Gary, the fisherman, was way too tough, and he had an angry side to his personality. He was big, strong, and handsome. I envisioned Gary throwing Johnny from the second story. Glad they left!

I provoked Gary once by smacking him in the face with a softball, which I could hurl at about 80 mph. So, he had a right to be pissed. He was way too strong and too much of a wrestler for me to handle. He swarmed me so quickly that I couldn't deck him with one of my knockout punches. He got me with a few good smacks, but luckily, I was able to cover up enough where he couldn't do any damage. Lucky for me that Lonnie and a few other toughs were playing b-ball with us that day and saved my ass.

Lonnie and Bob B. had no fear of anyone. Bob B. and I just barely knew each other but respected each other. He was one heck of a fighter. Bob was impervious to fear, and he could throw punches faster than anyone I've ever seen. He was an adopted lad who lived next door to Woody Hayes. We would have just short, casual encounters, and he was always very respectful and fun.

Then he just vanished. That has always left me wondering: what happened to this talented young man? My guess was that was sent off to military school like so many of our neighborhood malcontents. He was a good fellow with huge talents, and someone missed assessing that in him. Perfection would never be achieved by rejecting someone and them sending them to an arena that was designed to reconstruct you to be the perfect 'soldier'. We didn't need soldiers; we needed people with a heart and an understanding of the real world. The greenhouse surrounding us was starting to crumble; far too many realities were shining through.

We started spending a lot of our time either at the 11th Avenue apartment or on campus at the Thirsty I. One Friday evening, we had quite a gathering at the piano bar in the back. We were all singing, "Keep your balls rolling, keep your balls rolling, girl. The name of the game is fuck!" Stacie from Worthington joined us with a friend. She had to be one of the nicest-looking chicks in the north end, let alone the city. Well, we drank well into the night, and as it got later, she and I got really friendly. It was almost surreal, because this girl was so hot that over the years, each time I saw her, it conjured up images of just fucking her on the spot. She was like the north end enigma. She wanted to know all about playing in a band.

Stacie was real interested in whom I had met and who I played with. Finally, I suggested to her that we head to my place, and to my surprise, she said, "Fine. Bring your buddy Jon along." So be it. Off we went. Her girlfriend stayed behind because she had something going with one of the bouncers. She wouldn't get out of there until past 2:00 a.m. Straight to the apartment that was now equipped with many beds, couches, sofas, tables and all. Stacie, Jon, and I entered, and Jon went after some Stroh's. Her and I cuddled up on a couch and started mashing like there was no tomorrow. Frankly, I was shocked that a chick of this caliber was even with me. This girl, her looks, and style was the envy of many, and here she was, right in my arms and hotter than melted butter.

We mashed, caressed, sucked, licked, touched, manipulated and went on and on until she wanted Jon to join in. This was rather awkward, because I certainly wasn't into male, male, girl things, but hey, it was her call. She and Jon tossed for a while, as I backed off and had a beer. I'm not homophobic, and I didn't even know the word then, but I wasn't into guys under any circumstances. I wanted Stacie one on one. Jon enjoyed a quickie that was kinda sexy watching the two getting it on in the light of the Buck Moon.

There's something special about spontaneous, unbridled hedonism, hard body sex in the heat of the night. Especially after six or more Stroh's. It was surreal cause the gyrations were of two profoundly tan bodies and really only seeing were suits and clothes had been. So, after a beer, I moved back in and had some glorious sex with this pristine pussy. She had perky, soft, pointed tits. Her ass was to die for, and a flat stomach with abs that you grate cheese on. She ultimately had that Bo Derek look, and she was a turn-on whether she had clothes on or not. The reality was, and we knew it, that this was a one night stand, nothing more. This was a real damn shame, but Stacie had a line of beaus who wanted her so badly, that taking a number and standing in like just wouldn't be worth it. Plus, you'd probably have to fight some asshole about every other night, just to defend keeping her. This was not worth it.

Plus, she was more or less the sexual counterpart to Jon and me, and I don't think that'd who I would want as a girlfriend. We were too loose, and so was she! Unless you were there, you would have never known that deep inside this girl was nothing but passion and libido. We were probably safe for her. We could afford her an opportunity to have some great sex, and no one would ever really know. My only regret is that I couldn't make that night last any longer. Just being on top of her, with her tight little pussy totally engulfing my cock and staring at her luscious tits was enough to make anyone orgasm, which I did, and it seemed to last forever. Stacie too came with much force and a sense of relief. It was as though she had all of this sexual energy pent up inside her and now it was time to release it. When we parted for the evening, she just kissed me on the cheek and had us drop her off back at the I. She was planning on getting a ride home with her buddy. Never again did I see her or hear from her. Damn shame.

School was increasingly becoming more of a drag. The boring curriculum, the lack of freedom within the building, the inability to play any sports and rejection feelings that I was dealing with because of my breakup with Susie were all influencing me to just back off of everything. My classmates and many of my buddies were starting to turn 18 years old and now they had to register for the draft. Guys would receive their draft cards in the mail, and some would come to school with them and show them off. As if it was some kind of trophy. Shit, it was a death sentence.

It still puzzled me as to why in hell we were in Vietnam. Charles De Gaul of France had warned America to stay the heck out of Dutch Indochina. The

French had been there for more than a decade and accomplished nothing. So now, Big Brother America was moving in to supposedly stop the spread of Communism. Too much of the book 1984 was already coming to past in the sixties. These uncertain times caused me and many, much concern. There was also an internal ploy within the school that if you started skipping too much or in any way put your grades in jeopardy, the administration would contact your draft board and advise them of your status. This could result in an early call-up to serve in the armed forces. Some, like Gary, Mr. Freckle, decided to preempt that arm of power and he went down and worked out a deal with the Marines. He was to be inducted on July 1ˢᵗ at Camp Pendleton, CA. So, the countdown for him had begun.

We still had months to hang out, party, and just be friends. Our trips to the river to fish would undoubtedly disappear, and just the fun of playing baseball, catching snakes, and chasing girls would be things that would have to be put on hold very soon. Jon just went about his school life as if nothing really mattered. He had bad knees from football injuries, so he felt that he'd be bumped from induction if they did ever draft him. He started partying every day. I think that he went 29 straight days going to school drunk. That was quite a string and not something that you would necessarily expect from a guy who came from a six-pillar mansion, drove a dragster, and wore mostly designer clothing.

Thinking back on this, you just have to wonder, where the hell were the teachers when he'd fall in the door drunk and no one ever confronted that or even asked him if he needed help? Go figure! It was the same with so many things. Denial was the cloud over the sunshine of everybody's life. It didn't matter what your problem was, whether it was symptomatic of more complicated underlying troubles or the more obvious characteristics of substance abuse. The axiom was, if you played hard and helped the system to get accolades, then there was never a problem. This even transcended to the outer systems like the police.

Most of them stopped for various offenses. Sometimes, I was driving; other times, I wasn't. If there was beer in the car or if we were obviously drinking, the cops would just have you get out of the car and dump your booze. They would then follow it up with this stern warning, "If we ever catch you doing this again, off to jail you'll go!" Bull!

Shoot, we were having this huge motel party down by the Grandview Inn. Laura and Christie were there, the two girls from the north end who were always somehow attached to Greggo. They had arrived earlier than most, and I had the opportunity of jumping Laura's bones before the rest arrived. I was always amazed at her 34 DD tits. Man, they'd make any guy's dick do a dance. Plus, she was small, compact, and quite curvy, so she was a great sexual partner. She was not the least bit inhibited and so everything with her was fair game. That I liked, but I was always worried as to who she may have been with recently who might have a disease that they haven't even found a name for yet! Well, as the party got going and people came and people went, a knock on the door got everyone's attention at about midnight. It was the Grandview Police.

They were polite and courteous, but they wanted to know who had rented the room and they wanted IDs from everybody. Bummer! I stepped up to the plate and offered my ID to one of the officers. He shined a flashlight on it and said, "Are you Bob's kid?" With that, I responded, "Yes!" He went on to lecture me and ask if my parents knew what I was up to. I became quite apologetic and highly cooperative. He and his sidekick just said that it was time to wrap this up. "Dump your booze and go home." Within a half hour, all were gone except Greggo, Christie, and Laura. The cops left and the noise was gone, along with the cars. So, I figured, hey, why not? Laura was always game for another screw. So, off we went to bed, and that girl just about turned me into a prune by sunup. Man, she could jump and thump like no other, and she enjoyed the ride each and every minute. She drained me of so much fluid, I had to sit down to pee. Greggo gave the girls a ride home and came back to get me. I needed some sleep, so I seized the moment and got what I could.

It was back to our 11th Avenue pad for the afternoon and evening. Greggo came along, which was a good thing. He had been a friend throughout high school, but he attended Watterson. That didn't sell really well with some of my Golden Bear buddies. He did live in the uppity up neighborhood, and so, he was accepted. His dad was a racehorse vet and as Greggo would say, "He's been home 7 times in 8 years, that's why we've got 7 kids in our family."

Greggo always had the latest in super production fast cars. He had 400 CID Buicks, 442 Olds, and many others. He also had a 350 CID Camaro that would rip the ass off a dinosaur. He loved to drag race, and he loved to party. He was an excellent driver. I was with him so many times, and it seemed that when we were about to crash, usually going about 100 mph, he always swerved his way out of all predicaments.

At the apartment, it was a hot day, so we opened the roof-top windows and headed out onto the balcony to get a little sun. We got to know many of our neighbors that way. Gary, Mr. Freckle, was grilling mule deer steaks that had been marinated, and we were drinking Stroh's like there was no tomorrow. I had heard of a Grandview chick that had the hots for me, so I gave her a call. Lynn was quick to agree to come over for steaks, beer, and a good time. She was one hot little thing. Sexy little body, 32A or B cup boobs, tight waist, and a sexy face. We hit it off well, and she seemed to be a great distraction from my lingering pains of losing Susie. She was pretty conventional, and I remember that it just wasn't the thing to do to try and seduce her at that moment in time, but by the next weekend, I was spending the night at a friend's house, and she and I made love like there was no tomorrow. She was remarkably soft with wonderful breasts and a tight little pussy. We stayed very conventional, no oral sex, just straight up, kissy face, touchy bod, let me slide it in ya' kinda passion. It worked for both of us.

It was pleasurable, and it connected us at a higher level of interaction and commitment than we had previously. She was now becoming 'my girl!' Too bad I didn't share with her all of my other liaisons. This was the same little lady who I had at a CRO party when a classmate kissed her, and I nearly had to rearrange his face for it. This relationship of ours grew. It lasted for a period of time and if it wasn't for my inability to stay totally committed, we may still be together. Like so many things, wanting to break free from the hypocrisy of the culture we lived in and to somehow escape the inevitability of joining in on the Vietnam War, maybe things would have been different. Lynn dumped me in a very classy way. I appreciate her moxie and her creativeness. To this day, I still miss her; however, she caught me cheating!

Widening Down
the Senior Year

Gary, Jon, and I were getting increasingly tight. Jon really didn't give a shit about anything, because he felt that he did not have any 'national commitments hanging over his head'. His knees would be his way out. Gary was already signed up for the Marines for four, count them, four fucking years. I was in limbo, because my grades sucked, so did my attendance, and I had no idea what I wanted to do after graduation. I don't know what influenced me, or motivated me, but for some reason, I went after contacting my elementary school lover and seeing how she was doing. It wasn't all that difficult, but finally I was able to hook up with Mary on the phone.

I could tell that her mother was excited that I called, so that told me that she was hanging with the wrong crowd. Mary started writing to me immediately. She told me that she wanted me to visit Scottsdale, and when I responded, I basically told her that I was considering relocating to get the hell out of Golden Bear land. She responded and told me that she wanted me to come and stay with her and that it was okay with her mom. Man, that seemed strange, but hey, why not! So, Gary and I started talking about the notion of heading to Phoenix and saying, "Fuck the Midwest," and him saying, "Fuck the Marines." We still had much unfinished business at home, so this basically became a side-bar conversation. All the while, Mary continued to write and extend the offer to come live with her. She even threw in a few romantic tie-ins so that I might be enticed to visit.

The band was starting to dwindle as a sideline. All of us were faced with the decisions of growing up, getting married, going to college, or going to Vietnam. The latter obviously was the most unpopular. We were also becoming divided in our love of music. Some were into Dylan, that stinky little Bobby Zimmerman from Minnesota, then others were into the Stones and the new tunes from The Beatles. There would be no compromise. This now was becoming our life's blood. New groups were taking over, and there wasn't the time to figure out if Jim Morrison was the way to go or Van Morrison. There were bigger fish to fry, and our lives were about to take separate turns. Too bad, because we had a great future, but it was shattered by the nonsense and notion of the Vietnam War. We all had to fortify behind marriage, school, or possible desertion to Canada. Even if you went to school, you had eight semesters until your ass was grass. If you got behind on your grades, you were toast. Nothing looked too promising. If you did finish college and then enlisted, odds were that you'd end up a 2nd Lieutenant in some infantry group. Rumor had it that most of these guys got shot in the back by their own men. Kinda like Dinkmeyer in Animal House. There was really only one thing that we could do. Road trip!

As others set up dates for the prom and many were applying to colleges, Gary and I were working on how we were going to bust out of the Golden Bear façade and go take up a new life elsewhere. Sounded good, but we really needed to think through this notion. One night, while I was in my bedroom at my uncle's, I was talking with Mary in Arizona and also listening to Cassius Clay fight on the radio. I can't really remember whom he was fighting, possibly Ernie Terrell, but he always came out on top. I was thinking about this guy, who was on top of the world, and he had been making some major rumblings about his discontent for the war. It was even upsetting 'The Greatest's' life. Maybe he was going to go on a road trip or leave the country or something.

Cassius came from the opposite type of ghetto than us Arlington boys. He was from the poor, undereducated parts of Kentucky. He too had to be disillusioned with the nation's bullshit, no matter how successful he was in the ring. He went on to win that fight, and I continued to talk with Mary. She was so reassuring that it was okay to come live at her house and if I wanted to bring Gary along, cool, no problem. I had her put her mom on the phone. She was very polite and cordial. She invited me to come live with them, and she also affirmed that Gary was welcome also. Mary later shared with me that Phil's mom now lived across town from them, and she implied that her mother had moved on to other interests. Then there was Joni to consider. This was Mary's younger sister who was now a budding 17-year-old. She was still at their home and turning wild and crazy. I had always remembered her as a loud-mouthed little tattletale.

As the school year was winding down, there was much to do. There was a CRO/ORC party one spring morning on a school day, down on the banks of the Scioto. It was your average beer-bash. The only difference was, we all had to go to school afterwards. Bummer! I decided to go a different direction and started chugging with a cute, freckle-faced little lady named Jean who was in my art class. She had a great body, and she had a sexy way about herself. She and I just connected mentally, and before the party was over, we headed to her car, drove down the park road a way and started mashing really hard. Man, she had a great rack!

Lynn, my girlfriend, was headed down to Ohio University that weekend, so I thought, what a great occasion to spend some quality time with Jean. We messed around quite a bit for about an hour. Then it was time to face the reality of going to school. If the whole class didn't show up and there were over 600 students missing from the school, there would be hell to pay. So, she and I set a date for Friday night. If I remember correctly, we doubled with Jon and his new girl from Worthington named Becky. She was a high-class little lady, with a hugely successful lawyer dad and a socialite mother. We all went to pick up Jean at her home in old Arlington. I had been warned about her father, and once I got there, I could see why. He didn't even leave the kitchen to meet me, he just yelled. His thoughts were jumbled, and I think that he was welcoming me and kicking me out of the house at the same time.

Jean appeared at the bottom of the staircase. She made a comment like "Well, I see you met my dad!" And then, we were off. There were no detours. We went straight to a beer carry-out and then to the Olentangey Inn. Jon had gotten a room earlier, and we already had the key, and we went straight to our party abode. Jon and Becky left for a while to go get something. This gave Jean and I the perfect opportunity to reignite our sparks from earlier in the week at the sunrise beer-bash. Man, she was hot. To me, a red-headed lady with just a light glazing of freckles about her boobs is a great turn-on. Her body was that of an Irish lass. Her skin was quite white, red hair, lovely tits, which were probably 34C, a tight waist, and a curvy little ass. She was menstruating, so she wasn't so hot on the idea of having intercourse, but we sure covered the bases doing everything else.

I then went and got a bunch of towels from the bathroom, spread them out on the carpet and got her to come and lie down with me. We pulled a blanket down off the bed, and now, she was more inclined to have me slip my hard, hot, throbbing cock, deep inside her. We had a wonderful union together. She was a great lover, and it was obvious that she and I had a puppy love thing going on between us. When we were done, we both headed to the shower. She wasn't the least bit bashful. I think that she even said, "Do you want to share?" And we did. It was a whole new sensual experience showering with a cute redhead with a wonderful ass. I washed her back, and she even washed my privates. It then stepped up a notch and we again made love, in the shower, with the hot water running all over us, standing up. Having a second orgasm was new to me. It wasn't something that had happened before. Now I learned how to mix up the sexual scenarios to make it happen. It was an encounter that we would never forget; however, Jean and I ended up going our separate ways. The chance for a mutual reunion kinda reappeared years later, but during this period of our lives, she would go her way and I would go mine. There just wasn't the time to get a new fling going. Plus, I think that she was so much under the wrath of her father, that she didn't have much autonomy.

When Lynn returned from OU, she shared with me that she would be headed there in the fall. I could see the handwriting on the wall with this. However, she reassured me that all would be well between us. So, we continued our little courtship and made love and dated on a regular basis for the spring. Gary, Gary, Jon and I continued to rent the 11th Avenue apartment, and we were actually starting to become part of the neighborhood. That was a real education in how the other half live.

'Down in the Boondocks' could have been the theme song for this place. Billy Joe Royal hit it right on the head when he sang about the other side of the tracks. As the weather got warmer, we would randomly get involved in b-ball games with the local gang members back in the alley. They had their own set of rules, and it was rough play, but it was fun. Jon had his dragster in prime shape by then, and we usually played very near where it was parked. Many of these tattooed thugs, with missing teeth and 'mother' carved into their arms, would ask about the '34 Plymouth.

Jon would always give them the simple version of what powered it and what it could do out on the street. These gypsy mothers had other things on their minds. One night, we were coming out of the apartment. It was very late. Jon had Becky, and I had Lynn. We were all planning on heading home. We packed into the coupe and when Jon started it, we all got rained on by oil! Damn! Someone had stolen all of the chrome off of the dragster, including the chrome valve covers. What a fucking mess! The coupe had an open top and that oil had sprayed just about everywhere. Becky was going to die if she didn't get home, and she lived the closest. It was still a long way down High Street. Jon, half-drunk and also very headstrong, decided that it was best to just drive the car as it was. So, off we went. I think that when we arrived at Becky's mansion, all you could see was our eyes! We had to stop about three times to purchase more oil to replenish all of the Texas T that was spraying all over us. We all kinda looked like Al Jolson in makeup when we finally arrived at Becky's. We were just a carload of bright white eyes!

The next day, Jon spent a lot of time on the phone trying to run down new parts for the coupe. Gary and I just laid around Jon's bedroom as I plucked songs on the Gretch guitar, and we worked on our plans to skip town. The only hold-up we had was money. We checked plane, train, and bus tickets. The bus came up as being by far the best deal. Gary didn't have much money resources. His dad had been on a drinking binge for about the past two months and so he was no help. My allowance went through my uncle, so he monitored my money pretty closely. My only redemption was my electronic equipment. I had two classy guitars and two amps. All of my stuff was Fender, so it should sell in a heartbeat. I put out the word that I was going to liquidate all of my equipment to friends and guys in other bands. I also had quite a bank roll from band gigs, so I felt that we were in good shape to travel and relocate.

Spring break was coming, and so was Easter. I needed to make plans to visit my folks, but I hadn't followed through. During the course of a conversation with Rick, he volunteered to take me to West Michigan. I was like "Damn! That's mighty white of you!" So, once we got out of school for vacation, it was Good Friday, and we were off. Rick drove his 289 Mustang as if he was in the Indy 500. Holy shit! We got to my parents' house in about 5 hours flat. That was 320 miles from Columbus. This was during the days of 2-lane roads. There were highways in Michigan, but that was only half the distance.

Many tornadoes were up near my parents' house, and it was truly devastating to see what a storm like that could do. I remember Rick and I driving by a church that was literally cut in half. Trees were down everywhere, and the whole town was in a state of emergency. We visited for several days, enjoyed Easter dinner, and then we were off. I remember calling my dad to tell him that we were back in Upper Arlington, and he remarked that we'd only been gone 4 ½ hours. I just reassured him that there wasn't much traffic and we made good time. I think that we possibly set a land speed record on that return trip! During the trip, Rick kept talking about joining the Marines and that he planned on talking to a recruiter once we returned. He was rather scary because he was already way too 'gung-ho'. He could picture himself as a grunt, and he wanted to be right in the action. To me, that sounded self-destructive, but we could only wait and see what would transpire.

I finally turned 18, and there wasn't much to celebrate. Jon's dad had tickets to the latest George C. Scott movie 'The Bible'. Jon, his dad, and several of his brothers picked me up at my uncle's house, and off we went to see the movie. Normally, especially in a state where you could drink at 18, you'd go out and party and the beers would be on the house. I had to wait for the weekend to finally be able to party. The next day at school, I had to make the cold walk to the guidance office to register for the draft. Bummer! It was surprising how quickly your draft card showed up in the mail. The good news was that I had a student deferment at least for the time being. I also wondered how growing up in a strong faith-based family, who did not believe in war, could possibly affect my future draft status.

All of the seniors were caught up in what can best be described as 'senior class activities'. Colleges visits, loan and scholarship applications, planning for the prom, getting a tux, getting a date, reservations at a motel, booze and beer, summer travel, and work plans. Since Susie and I had pretty much hit the skids, I had to start thinking of whom I was going to ask. I didn't want to go for one of the puppies who I had been hooking up with. They were too young, and none would probably be able to stay out all night long. Jean was available and a great temptation, but I felt that Jean was looking for something serious and I wasn't. It wouldn't have been fair to her to do things that may inadvertently lead her on.

Then I came up with the perfect solution: go for one of the numerous chicks that I knew from Watterson. So, I did. I went and asked a real hot blonde honey named Penny. She was very excited when I called her, and it was easy setting up plans with her. All we had to do was choose a restaurant and then we were good to go. I had never had a date with Penny before. When we first started high school, she always had older, upper classmen, jock-types for boyfriends. She had an older brother, who was kind of a tough guy, so I just always treated her with respect and as a friend. Now most of those older guys were gone off to college or in Vietnam, so the competition had been reduced considerably.

I went over to visit her one day using Cindy's motorcycle. Wow! What a rack. Man, it had been a while since I'd seen this little blonde. She had really filled out, all in the bosom area! This was going to be an adventure. Possibly better than the ones that Bill and Ted took! This could possibly be called 'Journey Around the Nipple!' Gary and I continued our planning as far as jumping out of the life of being Golden Bears. We were still working on strategy, because we did not want anyone to know where we were headed. Gary was planning on reneging on his Marine enlistment, so his whereabouts had to remain a secret. I stayed in contact with Mary in Arizona, and her excitement about us coming there was increasing. It almost seemed too good to be true. Then Gary hits me with the facts of his pre-induction commitments. He was supposed to report to some Marine base sometime during the first week of June. Shit! This was when prom was scheduled. We were going to have to depart much sooner than we had originally planned. This was starting to happen all too fast!

School couldn't have become anymore of a drag, but I learned that once you turned 18 years old, you could get a job and use that as a co-op credit. Great! I went and met with my lame brain counselor, and he set my schedule so that I could get out of school at 11:00 a.m. Now I needed a job, but I wanted weekends off. So, I went to BBF. That's right, BBF. Burger-Boy-Food-O-Rama! What an experience! I guess this was where every loser, who was missing teeth, dropped out of school in the 8th grade or who may have married their sister worked. I got the prestigious job of doing just about anything and everything.

One character who I got a real kick out of was the cook, who had dropped out of Upper Arlington. He was '*the* cook'. When any of the teachers and especially if any of the administrators showed for lunch, George would kick into action. He would spray their French fries with Windex, and every so often, he'd actually take a bite out of one of their burgers and then wrap it up and put it in the bag. He didn't care. They all took their food as takeout, so he figured that they'd be long gone down the road before they noticed that their food had been sampled. This was a great setup for me. I just worked the middle of the day. One dollar and three cents was the starting wage! I figured that my take-home pay was about 86 cents per hour. A guy could starve to death on this.

You did, however, get 3 items for lunch pro bono. Their food was the same menu as McDonald's, so it was not the healthiest place to eat, but what the heck, it would tide me over until we finished up the school year and headed out west.

I finally got a bite on my musical instruments and amps. A recording dude called me and discussed buying all of it. This was the way I wanted it handed, so that I didn't have to sell off the stuff piece by piece. I took Cindy's motorcycle, with Gary on the back, over to this guy's apartment. He seemed to be an okay guy, but he must have read the desperation on my face. He started talking such low numbers for the literal thousands of dollars of band equipment that I had that I finally told him that he was insulting me. We left. However, about two days later, he called back, and his numbers were much more generous. I agreed to sell two amps and one guitar to him, but I was going to hold on to my metallic blue Jazzmaster. I knew a lead guitar player from another band that was looking for a vintage Fender, so I contacted him and made a good deal. So now, we were pretty well fixed for cash. We had to wait until the perfect time to vamoose. I packed a trunk, one left over from my dad's days in the army. Then I snuck out of my uncle's house. I filled it with a good balance of clothing and personal items. I figured that if we were going to be gone forever, then I was going to need a lot of shit. Gary and I kept our belongings over in Jon's garage where no one would ever pay attention to more stuff being in the already overcrowded mess that surrounded Jon's dragster coupe.

The wind-down for our class really became a wind-up. There was so much being planned, with the prom, CRO parties, spontaneous romps at the Olentangy Inn and even word about pending marriages. Wow! There were also bon voyage parties organized for some who either enlisted or drafted because of age and the fact that it took them 5 or 6 years to get through high school. Then, there was the annual CRO/ORC prank that had to not only be planned but also executed. I don't have a clue who did it, or when, but it was a great idea. I learned about it long after the prank had been successfully pulled off. When the school year ended, it must have taken a major size group of guys to literally haul in and place at the top of the second floor, a 25-foot tree stump that was about 3 feet in diameter. It was hollow and was subsequently filled with cement. I believe that to this date, that tree trunk was turned into a bench and still resides at the top of the center staircase at Upper Arlington High School. Home of the Golden Bears! Very classy! CRO '67 hits again!

Gary and I planned our escape on the same Friday night as prom. It seemed the most likely time to jump, because most of our class would be planning on being out all night. Our buddy Jon planned on making an announcement at the prom dance that two of our favorite comrades had decided to move on to a new life in a new part of the world, and to keep them in our thoughts and prayers. I understand that it took a while, but we all figured out who he was talking about pretty quickly. It had been too many years for anyone to realize that I had been having conversations with my past pubescent lover Mary, so Arizona was not considered by anyone. However, Canada via Alaska sure was.

Most concluded that we had left the country to avoid the Vietnam bullshit. Hell, morally, I totally objected to war as a means of solving any problem. I didn't need another country to live in to make that point. Gary was about on the same page, but he had signed up, so his ass was officially grass. This move was not just totally about the war. It was just as much about us realizing that the umbrella of protection afforded to us by the cloak of denial, ignorance, superficial relationships and life among the rich, famous, and those living under a façade was quickly ending. The Achilles Heel of the Golden Bears was beginning to show. We had a good run at being able to do as we pleased. We had lived life in a vacuum and frequently escaped any and all responsibility for most of our wrongdoings and were, as a class, heroes of the day. More than time to leave the proverbial greenhouse!

The one commitment that still hung over our heads was that damn apartment on 11th Avenue. Gary (Katman), Gary (Mr. Freckle), Jon, and I all headed over there on our 'skip day' from school. This was the unofficial day that seniors didn't show up for classes. Holy shit, the place was a mess, the dishes hadn't been washed in weeks, and there had to be 400–500 beer bottles lying about and up on the molding strips in the hallways, as well as each room. There was still plenty of cold Stroh's in the fridge, and Katman and Jon started hitting that stuff while Gary and I cruised to the nearest grocery store that we could find. We needed cleaning supplies. The apartment had a $50.00 security deposit on it, and we wanted our money back. If memory serves me right, it was my money!

When we got back, believe it or not, the place was in more shambles than when we left it. Jon and Gary had gone on an early morning drunken frenzy and taken a hammer and broken almost every beer bottle in the place. They had thrown all of the mattresses, tables, lamps and other so-called furniture out the back door, over the fire escape and onto the lawn. Then they were jumping from the second story fire escape onto the mattresses. Boys will be boys; however, I really expected the police to show up. They didn't, but we had to hustle and figure out how the hell we were going to get all of this shit out of there. All of us piled into the dragster and headed to the ARC. We figured that some of the seniors would be hanging out there.

I can't remember the name of the geezer who we ran into, but he had his parents' station wagon, so we promised him $25 if he'd help us out. Back to the apartment we went, and even this guy was amazed that we expected to put all of this discarded crap into his parents' fairly new wagon. Now mind you, wagons back then were as big as boats. They could hold a shitload. His even had a luggage rack. So, we figured we were good to go! It didn't take too long but before you knew it, all of the mattresses and the rest of the furniture that was laying in the backyard was stacked neatly in this monstrous wagon and kinda neatly up on top. There was only room for three of us in the front seat, so Gary, the geek and I piled in and headed toward a dump out by my uncle's house. This was great, because I was going to be able to take care of the closing down of the apartment, get my deposit back, and still be able to skip town all in short order. We left Jon and Katman at the apartment with the coupe figuring that they would finish cleaning up the broken class and all of the other stuff that needed cleaning, like the bathtub that was more suited for raising fish bait in as opposed to soaking your naked body.

Well, as fate would have it, Gary, the geek, and I took care of business. I had to pay to get us into the landfill, so I was short on cash, and I had to promise the geek that I'd catch up to him at the ARC and give him his money. This never happened. Jon and Katman did absolutely nothing except leave and go shoot pool at the Golden Eight Ball, so the apartment was still in shambles. I got a phone call from the lady landlord the next day, threatening all kinds of stuff. I told her that we were planning on cleaning up the various messes and that someone in the neighborhood had broken in and smashed a lot of glass. She just told me to blow off, that my $50.00 deposit would take care of having someone reliable take care of the situation. Fuck! Luckily for me, the only phone number that she had was for the BBF, where I was working, and I was in my last few days there. That would be the last I would hear from her. The party pad was gone, but the memories would linger. Overall, it was a good experience. While others, especially on campus, were preaching free speech, we were expressing 'freedom!' We had become the very living emojis for CRO '67!

Westward Ho!

Gary and I elected to take the Greyhound to Phoenix. It seemed to be the least expensive, and it would get us there in about 48 hours. There were no long goodbyes. We just packed up our stuff at Jon's and headed out. I had Jon later that day call my aunt and uncle and let them know that I was alright and headed to a new life. The geek who helped us to move from our 11th Avenue party pad was kind enough to offer us transportation to the bus station, and I figured that he wanted his $25.00, which I gladly paid him. He also arranged to deliver my band equipment to the dude who had purchased it. So, life was good, or so it seemed.

There was nothing quite like traveling on a Greyhound. They're big, comfortable, clean, and filled with people from all walks of life. We made it to St. Louis, MO the first night, and the driver stopped at a Greyhound bus station so that we could get some food and freshen up.

Holy crap! Gary and I checked out the menu at the diner in the station. What a rip-off. A hard-boiled egg, toast and coffee was like $7.50. Now we could see the pattern of profit. Cheap seats and a ton for food and anything else you may want to buy. A plane gets you to Phoenix in 4 hours and the bus takes you ten times that amount of time. Oh well, you live and learn, and as guys who grew up in a greenhouse with little or no exposure to the real world, we quickly realized that each mile we rolled along in that ground grabbing super cab, we were pissing away our money. At least we were not like the poor bums on the bus who knew nothing of American geography. Thankfully, we were educated enough to know what state we were in, what direction we were going and where all the major landmarks were. Heck, some of the cats on this vessel were shocked when we crossed the Mississippi River. We'd overhear statements like "I thought that river was in Mississippi!" Damn, ignorance is a dangerous thing.

Our ordination by fire was going to include many incidents like this. Dumb is everywhere, and it's reflective of a national school system that favors those who are going to succeed no matter what. Those who have had the experiences of two parent families, balance meals, numerous reading materials including newspapers, current events discussions, preschool and team sports opportunities and a huge awareness of the locations and directions of where the rest of the world is, who lives there and what's going on in that piece of the planet. It's sad to say that even way back then, the majority of the folks we encountered, both young and old, were learning and life impaired. Sadly, we were raised to believe that everyone was basically on the same playing field in life and that our competition was everywhere. Bullshit!

We were living our life in a bottle, ignoring the pain, suffering and needs of the greater masses, and taking our path to a life of success way too casually. This trip for Gary and me was far transcending just the need to start over; it was a rebirth for both of us. It was a whole new learning curve. Unfortunately, it only got worse as we ventured the many miles to Phoenix. Once you're out west and past the Mississippi and you headed toward New Mexico, the reality of the poverty, lack of mobility, paucity of educational programs and discrimination is a national embarrassment. We were traveling the historic and famed route 66, which even had a TV show named after it. It was the golden path to the land of opportunity in Orange County, California, and Los Angeles. Cookie Burns, a teen heartthrob and actor on the show, helped to make the road so famous.

Basically, Route 66 was just a two-lane slab of asphalt that went directly through some pretty dry and rough country. Hitchhikers were just starting to be a national phenomenon as we traveled west. At each junction and town, you'd see guys and gals all searching for rides out west. Many were headed to California. Most were looking to get to San Francisco and go to the Haight-Ashbury section of town. We were finally in Flagstaff, AZ, a mountainous little town, where one could sense the gross division of the haves and have-nots. I was at a drinking fountain at the bus station and a little Indian lady, who was holding a child, would not take a drink of water before I did. I was like 'bull' to this. I stepped aside and prompted her to go ahead, it was okay, so she obliged. She was as cute as a bug's ear, and I just smiled as she went about her business. This spoke volumes of where this town was at in its attempt to segregate populations.

I had seen far too much in my family dealings with the Negroes of Columbus and how they were limited in what they could do for work. I was just thankful that my two generations of Irish immigrants to the States were blessed with the humanistic side to offer good jobs, good wages, an open welcoming in a home of love and the sense to provide safe transportation home to ladies who were in this world to fend for themselves. The solidarity of the McNally clan was now more appreciated than ever before.

Gary and I were settled at Mary's house for about $2^{1/2}$ days after we had left Upper Arlington. We were dressed like folks from the Midwest because we had sweatshirts and long pants on. Holy crap, it was 108 degrees! Dry heat or not, it was hotter than hell and made you sweat where you thought that you'd never sweat in your life. Somehow, the karma in this house wasn't right. We were greeted with a rather toned-down, "How are you?" This was not the same energy that I sensed on the phone. There was little, if any, fanfare. Little Joni, the youthful mouth that had pestered me all the while I was with Mary years before, had grown into one sexy little bitch. She was by far the friendliest, and she seemed quite cool with the fact that we were at their house. Mary, on the other hand, was kind of a cold bitch and what the hidden agenda was surfaced on the first night.

Gary and I are seated in the living room, just trying to get a sense of things and the next thing we know, there is a carload of Mexicans outside in a car taunting us to come out and fight. I was game, Gary was game, but Mary's mom was quick to come to the front door and tell us to sit down. She summoned Mary and told her to go out and get rid of her friends. We could hear them yelling at us in a bunch of gibberish, and various taunts. I was more than willing to oblige but then I started thinking, "Is it a setup? Has Mary invited us there to make her probably boyfriend jealous so that she can win him back over?" Fuck! I was not going to become any part of a triangle.

This wasn't racial, it was macho. It could become racial very quickly. Gary and I decided that we'd just hang and see what happened over the days and weeks to come. We spent our days trying to figure out what we were going to eat in this house with no food. Plus, we'd watch soap operas and then head outside and chase lizards down the alleys. Joni would be around a lot because she often skipped school. She wore a bikini all of the time and she had a body to die for. I can't remember what brought us together, but one day she was sitting on my lap and her buddy was on Gary's. We played around a little, and she gave me the opportunity of removing her top and playing with her small but very perky breasts. She had great nipples, nice and round, with soft tops. I licked and sucked them and massaged her pussy from the outside of her suit. She was definitely a virgin and she wanted to keep it that way, at least for now.

Joni was hot and a real turn-on. It seemed to really excite her to be able to rub a guy's cock on the outside and feel the excitement and the hardness. She was going to be a willing participant soon, but we'd just have to see when. Luckily, Joni was 18 years old and very youthful looking. Mary was usually nowhere to be found. She was emotionally cool and had superficial conversations with us. Within days, we got some phone calls. The first was my father. He just wanted to confirm where I was. It then occurred to me that if Uncle Joe had checked his phone bill he would know very quickly where we were. Dad shared with me that Gary ProRock, a junior, had been hit by a car and died on prom night. Dad also pointed out that I had failed to tell my date I was not going to the prom. Bummer! To this date, I do not remember how I forgot to do that but what an ultimate slam. I felt very bad for her. So, I called. She was cool. I explained what had gone on and what we were up to, and she said that she totally understood, and that life was cool. We left it that if I returned to town, Penny and I would hook up. It seems to me if I remember correctly that her older brother got killed in the Vietnam War. That is so sad. He was a cool dude, an athlete and obviously someone who she cared for very much. He was like so many others, just older than us, he went to Asia and never returned.

After a few weeks at Mary's, we were starting to get the message that maybe we weren't so welcome after all. Food became so scarce that we actually thought that they were trying to starve us out. Our only port in the storm was Joni and her friends. However, she eventually confided in us that Mary was back with Hector and that they were going to get married. Fuck! This was certainly a turd in the punch bowl of our plans. So, we decided to venture out in Tempe and try and find some jobs. What we ran into was that everybody wanted your social security number. Well, there was no way Gary was going to use his cause he was on the brink of being called a deserter. They'd track him down in a heartbeat if he used any identifying information. Piece work, like harvesting, was more in California as opposed to the desert of Arizona.

We checked with Phil's mom, Mary's mom's reported ex-lover, to see if they were hiring lifeguards at her apartment complex pool. She said that she'd check into it, and then she invited us over for a swim and lunch. A homemade meal was wonderful and swimming in mostly a singles pool was like walking by a dessert buffet. Damn, there was some really hot pussy lining this pond. Not many got into the water. They just laid outside, covered in thick applications of coconut butter, and tanned their streamlined bodies. Gary and I both acknowledged that after seeing this smorgasbord of beaver, we needed to figure out how to remain in Tempe or Scottsdale. Our money was becoming low, and as the days rolled by, we knew that unless we hit something that helped us secure some income, we were doomed. I didn't have the electronics that I needed to try and break into a band and the fact that they need to use SSN numbers was killing us wherever we went looking for work. Plus, every potential employer wanted to see our draft cards to know our status. Fuck!

Gary alerted me one morning that we could possibly have a little frolic with Joni and her friend. These encounters were few and far between, but when that happened, man was it every man's dream come true. We usually were watching TV, and Joni and a buddy would show up from either the upstairs or coming in from having gone somewhere. They always had their bikinis on, and they'd start playing Monkee music and singing 'I'm a believer', which is truly a classic song. Eventually, I'd get Joni on my lap and Gary would venture off with her buddy to somewhere else in the house. Joni and I would do some short-term kissing and then I started to massage her breasts from the outside of her suit. She really got horned up and she rubbed my cock through my pants. This day, I thought why not? So, I removed her top.

She was kinda embarrassed at first and I asked her why. "Cause they're so small." Yes, her breasts were mostly nipple but what a turn-on. I then softly rubbed and teased her nipples until they became hard and erect. I then kissed and licked them, and once she became more comfortable, I sucked them. I paused for a second to unbutton my jeans and exposed my throbbing cock. I placed her hand on it, and she slowly started to stroke it in an up and down fashion. We continued to kiss, I played with her nipples, and I slid my fingers up the leg of her bikini and massaged her clit. She started becoming so wet that it was a turn-on. However, I knew that there was no way I was going to make love to this nubile. She was still a virgin, and I did not want to get her pregnant.

The more excited that she got, the more she grasped my cock. She stroked it as if she wanted to take it home with her. Then out of nowhere, I came all over her and myself. Much of my orgasm landed on her breasts, and this seemed to turn her on even more. She started massaging her own breasts and so I continued to finger fuck her until she constricted enough so that I knew she was having her own orgasm. Whew! That was an encounter of the third kind. We never did get it on after that. We never had the opportunity. Months down the road, long after we had left their house for good, she called me. She wanted me to fly her to where I was. Unfortunately, I had to decline, but to this day I regret making that dumb decision. That's not to say that Joni and I would have had any sort of lifelong relationship. We would have had something special and unique. Since Lynn was at OU, I was still rebounding from my loss of Susie, Jean was out of the questions and so was Stacie, Penny would demand a lot of work to make up for the prom, so Joni would be all fresh! However, my priorities were turning to dealing with school, draft, and having some cash.

Gary and I finally came to the realization that Mary's house offered no hospice, hospitality, or permanence. So, it was time to move. Gary decided that his best move to save his ass from Leavenworth Prison was to report directly to the Marines. So, he called his recruiter, who put him in touch with the powers that be. He got booked on a jet going directly from Arizona to Camp Pendleton, California. I called my folks, who were more than happy to bail my ass out if I would fly directly to West Michigan and get a job and go to college. Fine! I can never erase my vision of Gary waving goodbye to me as my jet gained altitude flying out of Phoenix. I knew from that moment on, our lives would be changed. Here's the guy who used to buy The Beatles records with me, dance the twist, chase girls, go fishing, catch snakes, drink Stroh's and the one who gave me a Ted Williams 32 oz. bat for my birthday that helped me to become a baseball superstar. Our lives would now go separate ways. It would never be the same again.

We had never had a fight or disagreement. He was always my friend, even when I joined up with Tom D. to check out the freckles on his ass. I had known for far too long that even though he was a cool guy, handsome, and a friend, his life couldn't have a happy ending. His dad, who was an engineer, would disappear for months. His mother, although kind and holy, was inadequate, and his brothers were party monsters. Gary's life was going to be tough. I still loved him. Our plans to re-settle and establish ourselves only proved to us that we weren't capable of doing that. We were too dependent on the system to bail us out. Now life was really going to bear down on us.

Saying goodbye was one of the most difficult things that I ever had to do in my life. No, this was more like Janis Ian's words, 'Life Beings at 17.' So, hold onto your self-concept, convictions, and jock straps, because this was going to be the rollercoaster ride of your life. Sure, there are many pseudo relationships, those bound by work, situations, and other highly superficial passings, but with Gary, it was all 'legit' as Hammer would later say. "It was too good to quit." However, we were left with no choice. We were not in control, and we had to relinquish our control to other entities in order to get our lives straight. My only fear at that time was Gary would be headed to the rice patties. I would be headed to the blackboard jungle to try and stay the hell out of Asia. Ultimately, I wanted the freedom to head to Ann Arbor to possibly hook up with Seger, but the draft would not afford anyone that autonomy without a deferment.

Back in the Midwest

I had a pretty uneventful flight to my parents' home in West Michigan. All of my stuff was there, apparently, because my dad must have picked it up during one of his many travels through Ohio. There were no lectures, punishments or 'I Told you So's'. Life just went on like I had never left. However, now I was stuck in the great white north, and I was supposed to get my life together. My brother was coming home from the seminary with a couple of friends. He was going to stay and work during the summer at my dad's lumber mill. The house my dad had bought was large and in a prestigious neighborhood, and it was filling up quickly. My grandmother still lived with us and so did my two sisters. My brother and his buddies showed up on a Friday evening, so we had kind of a family get-together with barbeque and all the fixings. My dad had always loved cooking chicken on the grill using the rotisserie. Like most Irish families of the times, no one went without a drink. It never really mattered what your pleasure was, you just needed a drink. I came from the camp of beer drinkers and had never really drunk anything other than beer. My sisters were too young to drink, and my brother and his friends were all into Michelob. My parents stuck with their martinis, and they even had a dog by that name.

My brother's guy and gal friend were planning on staying until Sunday, and then they were off to Columbus. As fortune would have it, I got a call from Jon. He was checking to see if I was back at my parents' new home. He could sense from the tone of my voice or my lack of normal excitement that I was trapped. He told me he'd call me back. Within an hour, he called back and said that his dad was okay with me coming down and living with them. He also said that his dad had a job for the two of us and that I could live at their house as long as I pleased. This was almost too good to be true. I quickly explained to my folks my intentions, and I didn't see any excitement in their eyes. My dad just commented, "Well this now puts you completely on your own." So be it.

It wasn't hard saying goodbye to Dad, Mom, sisters, Grandma, or my brother. My gypsy side was starting to grow wings, and I had no connection with the great white north. No campus, no friends, no young person's bars or clubs, and too much at-home supervision. So, off I went, along with my brother's two OSU buddies and straight to Upper Arlington, the home of the Golden Bears. Maybe it was time to reignite the CRO '67 festivities! Jon's home was a familiar place, since we had spent literally hundreds of hours there during our last two years as CROs. I felt welcomed by all of Jon's family and his parents. Our job was going to be painting the complete inside of a home that his dad had purchased near the OSU campus. It was right up the street from the Thirsty I. Damn, what good luck! The house was huge. It was one of those 1920s large brick homes, with massive rooms, 12-foot ceilings, 6 bedrooms, a dining room with sliding pocket doors, several fireplaces, and a very impressive kitchen. The basement was dry and large, and it even had several concord grapevines growing in the backyard. This was a gargantuan project. Jon and I shopped with his dad at the downtown Lazuras Store to order all of our painting and wallpaper removing supplies. He got us ladders, sandpaper, steamers, paint, brushes, and all of the stuff we would need to totally spruce this place up. It was his intention to get it done in the summer so that it was ready to rent to a bunch of college kids by fall.

Jon and I developed a great routine in short order. We'd work from early in the morning while it was still cool outside, then we'd nap for an hour or so in one of the several beds or couches that had remained on this property. Then we'd get up, get showered, and get down to campus to look for action. On some nights, I would connect with Lynn, although we didn't talk much about it. She was headed to OU in the fall, and no matter what she would say, I would be left out of her life after that. She was far too cute, sexy and fun to be with, to think that she'd head down to one of the biggest party schools in the Midwest and act like a nun. No way! For the time being, she was the perfect girlfriend. She might have been from the other side of the tracks, so to speak, but she made up for any cultural deficits with good looks, a great body, and a sense of humor. She was never a bore, and physically, she was a total pleasure to make love to. We never did anything kinky, and all of our sexual encounters were pretty straight-up. However, each was special because she was a great lover, and she could be satisfied. Lynn was not inhibited, and when she had an orgasm, you knew it and she'd tell you. Shyness was not one of her qualities.

Frankly, it made me feel like I was a man, because all the while that I would be sucking on her nipples and stroking her clit and having her straddle me on top when she collapsed into my arms, I knew that she was satisfied. I too could them come and know that we had shared something very special together. Lynn was a very special person; however, the reality was that eventually, her life would go one way and mine would go another. This was sad, because for those special moments in time, we shared love, fun and companionship, and we never fought; we just laughed.

By July, the grapes behind the rental house were getting pretty ripe. I used to play chess with this guy named Andy who was the older brother of a girl I knew. He explained to me how we could make wine. So, one day, Jon and I got the bright idea of making wine. I forget how we obtained a 5-gallon jug, but with that some sugar, yeast, and a whole lot of squishing, we filled the jug with some very dark, purple grape juice. Andy told us that it would take about three months before the alcohol would start to ferment from in the juice. Great! Jon was spending an increasing amount of his time working on the '34 coupe. He now had it custom painted metallic blue. He also added white side pipes and headers. He had a plexiglass top installed, and his windshield and side windows were new, and they even worked! He had all of the stolen chrome replaced, and the car was looking totally cherry. He had new tires and slicks as well.

Jon was getting concerned that he kept reading and hearing on the news that Route 66 was going to be changed to another highway. It was no longer going to be the main pathway to the west. He was getting caught up in the nostalgic side of having a coupe, which should be for cruising 66. Now the road is going to be changed to something like Interstate 40. That isn't cool. Plus, the new road would be much farther north. It seemed that the old 66 was going to become a two-lane country road with no special fanfare. He started to talk about a trip out west. It was going to be the grand finale. The more he talked, the more serious he got. We received a letter from Gary, and he was in boot camp at Pendleton. He was hating every minute of it, but the fact that he was out in California got Jon even more hyped as to a Route 66 trip. Jon also wanted Route 66 signage. He and I were quite skilled at taking highway signs, because we had taken enough off of Ohio 290 to complete the floorboards in his coupe. We always had the right set of wrenches around.

One night at the North Berg, a bar on the north end of High Street near the OSU campus, a lot of the CROs and ORCs were hanging out. Maggie, a lifelong friend and a girlfriend to my buddy Mark, who was Gary's cousin, introduced me to Rita. A beautiful-looking blonde with great tits and a very nice ass. She smiled a lot, but she really didn't have anything to say. She spent most of that evening bullshitting with me in a booth at the bar. Then I get the warning from Hickey that she's Posey's girlfriend. Holy shit, Posey was a monster. He fought anyone, any place and at any time. Usually for no reason. I was headed to the pisser and lo and behold, who the hell was at the bar but Posey. Fuck!

Well, I went and took care of business and figured that the best defense would be an aggressive offense. So, I approached him. I figured he had to know who I was, either by reputation or whatever. "Hey Dick, how's things going for you?" "Why?" was all he said. Great, now I'd ran out of words and before I could say anything else, he chimed in, "I see that you're spending time with Rita." I was thinking to myself, *holy fuck, now I have my hands full. He probably outweighs me by 75 lbs. I may be okay if I can use my speed, I just can't let him grab me.* He then looks at me and mutters, "Listen, Mac, that bitch is crazy. If I were you, I'd be real careful dealing with her." "I thought that she was your girl. I've just been talking with her because Maggie introduced us." "No, she was my girl, but after several nights of her sticking her tits in my ears and then not fucking me, she's history." He then concluded "Mac, best of luck."

Whew! I was off the hook with him. That was trouble that I did not want, and I knew that I couldn't probably handle. He was one tough, very volatile hombre. The world then became a small place. After I returned to the booth and Rita and I were bullshitting, I came to the realization that she was Andy's sister. I knew Andy's younger sister but not this one. Shit, they were both cute as hell and supposedly a lot of fun. Well, Rita and I had one date on the weekend of the little and big sister weekend at OU. Lynn was down in Athens for that, so I seized the moment to spend some time with a new acquaintance. We doubled with Greggo and Christie, and we basically drove around, did some drag racing on High Street, and ended up at several bars. It was a very hot night in Columbus, and Rita got the idea that we should go skinny dipping. Damn, maybe she *was* crazy!

Well, off we went to Griggs Reservoir at about midnight. There was no one around, and we ventured down to the riverbank to just about the area we checked on Gary's freckled butt. Rita got naked almost immediately, and by the moonlight, I could see that she had a body to die for. Great tits, a tight slim waist, long blonde hair, large nipples that were hard and erect from the cool breeze off of the water, and a furry bush. In we went, and that water did feel refreshing but the shit on the bottom of the river just about scared each of us to death. Broken bottles, boards, nails, creatures, bones, boat parts and other paraphernalia that no one wanted between their toes. Snakes and muskrats were also cruising the shoreline and didn't make the experience any more pleasurable.

I tried my best to maneuver Rita to an isolated spot in the water, so that Greggo and Christie were alone and so were we. It worked, and Rita responded well to some hugging and touching. Posey forewarned me, she came across like a lady in heat who wanted to be fucked now, hard and several times, but as we proceeded to get more intimate, she kinda shoved me away. Strange! This was her romantic profile throughout the rest of the night. We were parked at a red light, sitting in the back set and the next thing I knew, she is unzipping my pants. She exposes my cock, slides it into her mouth and then starts sucking me off like there's no tomorrow. As soon as I tried to unbutton her blouse and lower her jean shorts, the gig was up. She quit and then acted as though I was moving on her too quickly.

Strange! I felt that if Jon and I did head west and Lynn moved to OU, then I'd better keep my options open. So, I thanked Rita for an enjoyable evening, gave her a brief kiss on the lips and promised to stay in contact with her. I also saw her sister when I dropped her off and we had a much more natural and realistic relationship. However, it was platonic. I wished her well and told both of them that I'd stay in touch.

Back West

It didn't take long, but Jon was well along in his plans to hop on 40 west and catch up to 66 and then make the circuit in LA and throughout California. One evening, we were cruising down Route 33, and I would guess that we were going somewhere between 130 and 140 mph. Jon was testing just how gutsy his coupe was. Well, out of nowhere and all at once, all of the glass in the coupe shattered. I was very glad that it was plexiglass. Otherwise, we would have been cut up like a slab of bacon in a butcher shop. Shit, when the coupe caught that rush of air, I thought that we were going to go airborne. Lucky for us, we didn't. It took the better part of 2 or 3 days to get all the glass replaced and installed. Now Jon was more determined than ever. He wanted to pack and pack lightly, jump in the coupe and race toward Indianapolis so that we could visit his uncle and hook up with Route 66. Like the Phoenix trip with Gary, there were no long goodbyes. As a matter of fact, we just picked a day, and off we went. This was very spontaneous. In true CRO '67 style, go for the gusto, worry about the consequences later!

It isn't all that far from Columbus to Indianapolis, and what we noticed in the initial leg of our journey was a huge number of hitchhikers. Man, they were everywhere. The hippie culture was emerging at a geometric rate. Chicks had long hair, no bras, numerous beads, and now there was this new high coming out of Vietnam called 'weed'. It had to be a Frank Lucas plot to make money, however, New York had nothing to do with the Midwest. Neither Jon, I, or any of our friends were into this new shit. We still were Stroh's men, but very soon, we'd be doing Coors as we crossed the Mississippi.

We did have one close friend, David, who was very much involved with the SDS. He was buddies with Abby Hoffman, and we were certain that David and his wild-ass, anti-authority friends were doing grass as much as they were doing Raisin Bran. So, by cultural standards, the rules of the inner city and the changing times, we were conservative. So many back-home thoughts that we were wild-ass spoiled rich kids. Yes, we were, but we were also just out for cheap thrills and a geographic experience that one could tell their grandchildren about. This massive movement out west was stimulated by free speech, new drugs, a falling-out campaign and the promise of free love. CRO '67 forever, or so we thought!

There was so much change and challenge at this time that it was hard to separate what one was going to focus on. We had the LSD invasion being brought on by a so-called Timothy Leary. The SDS, who was hell-bent to cause chaos in response to this Asian conflict that no one would call a war. There were vibes that we were mere months before a man would be on the moon, and we were faced with having to sever ties with our comrades from the ranks of the Golden Bears because we were moving in a new geographic direction. Separation is never easy. If it lasts, it's a loss. Tough to deal with when one is only 18 years old.

Those first 18 years were quite an experience, and I think that both of us wondered what the next 18 would hold for us. We made it to Indianapolis, but that damn coupe started having overheating problems. Man, this was an age-old problem that took us out of the 4th of July parade a year ago, and here we go again. We made it to Jon's aunt and uncle's house, and we just placed the coupe in the garage. It was steaming like a locomotive, so we just left it alone.

This was a pretty typical mid-western, middle-class family. They lived in a nice house, in a nice neighborhood. There oldest child, a cute girl, was 17 years old. They also had a son, but he was a chaser. He was about 10 years younger than his sister. We didn't hang around too long but long enough for trouble to brew. Jon took off with his cousin to go to a beer-bash and bonfire one night. I hung around the house because I wanted to watch something on TV. Jon and his cousin returned by about midnight and Jon looked beat up. He had a split lip and a black eye.

"What the fuck happened to you?" I asked.

"Well, the toughest guy in the school thought that he'd try and show his buddies that he can take on anybody. So, I obliged him."

"And you lost," I responded.

"Kinda!" was Jon's only remark. Well, like teens everywhere, when you mix groups, they all go pissing on each other's fire hydrants. It was evident that this was not nirvana and time to move on. The only problem was, we didn't have any wheels. So, we finally decided that 'when in Rome, do what the

Romans do'. So, we packed to continue our journey by hitchhiking. We bid farewell to Jon's relatives, and we bummed a ride from his uncle to the interstate. Off we went. Again.

Jon was growing a beard and so was I. We were wearing jean jackets, and I think that we both had bell bottoms on that fit very tight on our asses. My hair continued to get longer, but it was so curly that it was often hard to tell. I had on a surfing T-shirt, and Jon just had a plain colored tee on. We each had a backpack, so now we at least looked the part to join the other dozens of hitchhikers vying for a ride west. Getting rides was not that big of a deal. You just had to be careful whose car or truck you entered. Some hitchhikers mysteriously disappeared over the years. The girls, especially the braless, let's-smoke-weed-and-everything's-cool gals often got raped and then dumped somewhere, hopefully without their throat slit.

We would travel by day and then find places to sleep at night. We had sleeping bags in our backpacks, and they proved to be very useful. It didn't take all that long, maybe two days, and we were in Oklahoma. We got picked up there by a mid-twenty-year-old Latino who talked as if he was the toughest guy on the planet. I know that his name was Ray, but I wasn't totally sure of his last name. He told us that he was on R&R from Vietnam and that he had been visiting his sister and was now headed back to Pendleton. Perfect. He could drop us off in L.A. What was strange, though, was that he was driving a station wagon, and it was filled with all types of household belongings. Toasters, ironing boards, clothes and tons of other shit. This stuff was just crammed into the back and back seat of the wagon. All three of us occupied the front seat.

There was a lock on a chain in the front seat. The lock was a USMC issued lock, so we figured that he was a Marine, and he was probably moving his family to the base. We did find room for our backpacks and sleeping bags in the backseat, but our coats, along with his green army fatigue jacket, were in the front. We traveled together for about one and a half days. We talked a lot, and we switched drivers, so we did our sleeping in the wagon. If bullshit was people, Ray would have been China. This guy had more stories than anyone. They all revolved around how tough he was. We were in a coffee shop in Gallup, New Mexico one morning, and for some reason, he got into this scrap with one of the locals. It took both Jon and I to drag his sorry ass out of there before the cops came. I think that a 'dirty look' was what instigated the near melee, and we would have ended up taking on the whole town if he had started any trouble. Ray didn't see it that way, and he perseverated on the notion of going back and kicking this guy's ass.

It was about sunset, and we were cruising through Flagstaff, Arizona. I was sleeping on Jon's shoulder with both of our coats rolled up and serving as a pillow between us. Ray was just constantly babbling but no one ever really listened. Jon, I think, was half asleep, leaning against the car door and window. Ray made some sort of comment about police, and I think that Jon and I each opened one eye and just perused the area around us. Well, we had a cop car on each side of us and behind us. Ray made some lame comment about "Hey, we have nothing to worry about…" Well, was he ever wrong. This was where the bullshit stopped.

These police pulled us over in a parking lot and literally pulled us out of the wagon. As Jon and I were removed from the front passenger side, out came our coats onto the ground. Ray was spread-eagled on the hood, and Jon and I soon followed. One of the cops was going through our coats and backpacks. He then rolled 3 or 4-dime store quality switch blades onto the hood of the car, plus he threw the chain and lock from the front seat on the hood. "Whose weapons are these?" he asked. We all kind of just looked at each other, hoping that Ray would explain that he told us that he was coming from Mexico where he had purchased some cheap knives to resell. Plus, the lock was from his Marine Corps locker. He didn't say word one.

Next thing we hear is that Ray is being read his rights and the cop is stating that he's driving a car without the permission of the owner, that he is an unlicensed driver and that these weapons are considered concealed. Fuck! We, too, were handcuffed and thrown into the back of the cruiser. One officer asked us how we were connected with Ray, and we told him that he picked us up while hitchhiking. The cop replied "It's against the law to hitchhike. You are probably vagrants, and carrying a concealed weapon is a crime." Fuck! As they escorted Ray past us to put him into another cruiser, he looked at us and said, "Guys, I'm not really in the Marines." Well, doesn't that beat all? Mini John Wayne was a fucking sociopath, felon, psycho and now were connected with him. Plus, it was a Friday night! Now we knew we'd be in jail till Monday for sure. I'd never heard of a judge that worked weekends. Long hair, hippies and surf bums were considered the scum of the earth. We were fucked!

Ray was placed in a cell with beds and only a few other inmates. Jon and I ended up in the drunk tank with about 30 other lost souls, one toilet, and naturally no toilet paper. The floor was damp and cold, and there was barely enough room for anyone to sit down. There were no benches, seats, or beds. Just a big room with high ceilings and large bars that separated us from the real world. This was some sort of wake-up call. Jon and I were still in a daze from what had happened out on the street. After about 3 hours, we were each taken out of the cell and escorted to a booking room.

There, a cop searched us, took our photos, and fingerprints. I asked this cop who was filling out forms and standing at the counter in the room as to why we were being held. He replied, "Well, for starters, you and your friend are party to no driver's license." I tried debating that reality with him, but he just said, "Tell it to the judge! The other crime is that you were carrying concealed weapons." Again, I explained to him the reality that we had been picked up by this 'Ray' guy in Oklahoma. He was the one with these so-called weapons in his car and we assumed that he owned the car and had a license. "Tell it to the judge!" was his response. With that, he walked away.

We also got to make phone calls, so I called Rita, and Jon called a chick who liked him who worked for his father as a wig stylist. We requested that they wire us as much money as they could to get us out of jail. There was no telling when we would see a judge and if they would end up bonding us over for a criminal hearing, we could be there for a very long time. Long hair, with surfer shirts, bell bottoms and beards were not welcome. That message came across loud and clear. It gave us a new appreciation for how minorities are treated everywhere on a daily basis. Here we were, the spawns of highly successful people, and we were being treated like dogs.

It turned out to be a long three days before we finally saw Judge Roy Bean, the hanging judge of Arizona. That really wasn't his name, but that's what the crowd in our cell called him. We needed humor to survive those 72 hours. Damn, there were some really bad people in the cell with us. One big black guy was in there for killing someone with his fists, and the Indians who came in were drunk and subsequently were beaten up by many of the others who weren't Indians. What a sad world. It was a place of hate. The inmates hated each other. The cops hated us all. Society wanted us out of sight and out of mind, so they could go about their so-called normal lives. To a lesser degree, it was like in Upper Arlington; the only difference was, we would undoubtedly be treated harshly so that eventually we'd leave this town and never come back to it again.

Going back to being a Golden Bear seemed awfully attractive. Especially after three days of watching fights, avoiding getting assaulted, sleeping on a damp floor, and smelling people who hadn't taken a shower in months. This was not the lifestyle we were used to. Well, we each went to see the judge by mid-day on Monday. We had received $100.00 in money from Jon's friend, and interestingly, we were each fined 45.00 for the knives and the driver's license issue was dismissed. I tried debating the whole concealed weapons deal with the judge and he said, "You'll have to take it to court, consult with an attorney, and wait for a jury hearing. It will take about 2 months for that to be arranged." Well, that was enough for me to plead guilty and pay my fine and get the hell out of dodge! Jon was right on my heels.

We got out of the jailhouse by about suppertime, and we headed to the Western Union Office. Jon shared with me that he had more money coming but that he did not want the police to know that we had it. Otherwise, they would have fined us more. We figured that they had a nice little scam going on there. They book a person for some marginal crime, let you rot in the tank for a few days, and then offer you a deal to get out as long as you have some money. Otherwise, you stay in jail and wash cop cars and do lawn work in the Arizona sun for about a month. After we got several hundred dollars more, we checked into a small motel along Business 66. We each took showers, changed clothes and definitely used the bathroom! Then, we went to a diner, ate a meatloaf dinner, and then we were back out on the road, hitchhiking west. We hadn't hitchhiked at night before, and it wasn't totally dark yet, but we wanted out of that town like now!

We got picked up by a couple of real hippie dudes right away. They wanted us to drive, so after we switched seats, Jon ended up behind the wheel of their old Ford Galaxy. These guys were like Cheech and Chong and highly suspicious. They had something that they kept talking about between them, but I never fully understood what the hell they were saying. It was getting pretty dark, so Jon flipped on the car lights. Soon, the headlights started going from low beam to high beam. They were doing this on their own. Jon played around with the floor button that controlled the lights, but the problem persisted.

We finally pulled over to check what needed to be checked because he was definitely Mr. Motorhead. He asked for a screwdriver, and one of the dudes said he thought that they had one in the trunk. We all went back to the trunk, but for some reason, one of them said that Jon and I should stay with working on the motor, and they'd get the tools. That seemed strange. Well, they fiddled with the trunk lid for a while, but it did open. I got a quick glance of what was in the trunk, and it was just what I didn't want to see. These dudes were shipping drugs.

The trunk was packed with reefer and our two backpacks. This was just what we didn't need or want. Holy shit, we just left the land of Wally and the Beaver, and now were going to get a front row seat to see Johnny Cash at Folsom Prison. Jon was unable to fix the lights. He figured that if he disconnected the high beams, then we'd just drive the rest of the way in low beam. Great idea, but it didn't work. We were still under the hood, and I told Jon what I saw, and he looked at me and whispered, "We've got to get the hell away from these assholes!" We drove all the way to Needles, California with those damn lights going on and off.

The reality is, there isn't much between Flagstaff and Needles, just a lot of deserts. Jon pulled the car off on a side street and told the hippie dudes that he was going to work on the lights again. One stayed in the car, and the other went to open the trunk. Jon and I stayed up by the front of the car until this dude had the trunk opened up. They had the trunk rigged somehow so that it took two keys to open it. When evil dude came around the car with the screwdrivers, we walked the opposite way back toward the trunk. We grabbed our stuff and off we went. You would have thought that a junkyard dog was chasing our asses, but we were gone. After we traveled 3–4 blocks and crossed a few main streets, we saw a small motel with a 'Vacancy' sign flashing. We headed straight there and checked in. It was like $7.00 for the two of us for the night, because the lady said it was so late. It sure was a good feeling to have gotten away from these drug running criminals. So, as we crashed on nice comfortable, clean beds, we both remarked how it would be nice to get back on the road again in the morning and be more selective as to who we rode with!

As luck would have it, things planned seem to never go exactly as they are expected. We took some back streets the next morning and headed across a piece of desert to get back to Route 66. We were geeked. Now we were in California. The worst, or so we thought, was behind us, and now it was to the land of oranges, beautiful ladies and a whole lot of beach. We both realized that being a Golden Bear, no matter what gene pool you came from or who were your neighbors, or what your dad did, had little if no value on the street out here. We were on our own, and to our unfortunate luck, we had a criminal record. I suggested to Jon that we would contact F. Lee Baily once we got back to Columbus and have him file suit with the neo-Nazis in Flagstaff. However, that was so 'Golden Bear'. Here I am thinking of who the best legal ass-kicker on the planet is, and I'm living day to day basically off of the street. Reality still had not sunk in.

I'm not exactly sure where we were between Needles and Bakersfield, but it was the middle of the day, hotter than hell and we were perched under some sort of rotten tree by 66 for some shade. We had gotten a couple of short rides, but nothing that was going to take us deep into Orange County. I'm not sure who saw them first, but we both reacted the same. Run!

Damn, coming down 66 headed West was that old Ford Galaxy with the evil dudes. It was on a curve, and we both headed south, through the tangle of dried wood, dead trees, and a shit load of sand. We both jumped over a large tree trunk and hit the dirt. Whew! They drove by. We thought for sure that they had seen us and that would have escalated their paranoia, but they must have missed the blur of us hauling ass through the brush, so we did not have to deal with these criminal assholes.

These two were Charlie Manson lookalikes. Their personalities were at about the same level. We knew that we had to distance ourselves from them, any way possible. We just slowed our westward movement. We hitched a ride to some small town, where I remember the temperature at about 7:00 p.m. was 100 degrees in the shade. So, we settled into a diner that had a supper special that we bought, plus several iced teas. We decided to sleep back behind a huge road sign that night. Surprisingly, it got rather cold, which was a relief. The next morning, we were up early and ready to go. We hooked up with a driver who was headed back to Pendleton after a stint in Vietnam. Damn, it was like running into Ray all over again. This guy seemed to be on the up and up. He was articulate, he had his uniforms with him, and he didn't talk crazy. So, we thought that we just may get to the ocean yet and start enjoying the California lifestyle.

The End of Route 66

We were riding in a late model T-Bird, which Sarge, our new buddy, said belonged to his mother. It sounded good, so we didn't question where he got the car. He was supposedly from New Jersey, and he had the accent to support that. Our first stop, once we made it into Orange County, was naturally orange grove. None of us had ever seen one, and they were quite impressive. Literally, oranges were everywhere, and boy did they ever look yummy. So, like many others had probably previously done, we pulled off onto a two-track that led into the orchard and exited the car.

We each went different directions, and we used our shirts as a way of collecting a large bundle of freshly picked oranges. We all got back to the car rather quickly because we knew there had to be some laws that govern the illegal picking of fruit. As we got back into the T-Bird and tossed all the oranges into the back seat, as one might expect, here came an old pickup truck, loaded with farmhands, screaming something, so we knew it was time to get the hell out of there. Thank God for the power behind a T-Bird. This car screamed its tires. We reversed and got the hell back on the asphalt and down the road in mere seconds.

The pickup was still bouncing down the two-track, and we could have sworn that the guys in the back had shotguns! Sarge had that Ford up to about 100 mph in the blink of an eye, and soon, we were able to merge with the intrastate highway, and our days on 66 were quickly coming to an end. We were now headed to the Pacific Coast Highway, and our destination was just water and sand. Call it fate, karma, or luck, but we somehow ended up in Newport Beach. Seeing the ocean for the very first time was exciting. I had to go jump in just to see what saltwater was all about. It was the perfect place.

Newport Beach is blue water, volleyball courts on the beach, cute chicks and numerous beach houses. We stopped at a place called the Bal-Broaster and had a seafood dinner. It was fabulous. Then we headed south, down the main drag, to find a place to stay. We crossed over into Balboa, the south end of Newport, and checked into the Balboa Inn. Nothing fancy about this joint, but the couple who owned it were hip and the rates were reasonable. Plus, Sarge was footing the bill for the first two weeks.

Now we had a feeling that all of our efforts, sacrifices, torture, bad deeds, and horrible experiences had been worth it. We were completely denying the realities of the fact that the draft was hanging over our heads but in typical Golden Bear fashion, 'who cares!' We'll get bailed out somehow. The hippie crooks were long gone, and the irate farmers had lost in the pursuit of the fruit hungry tourists. Yes, those oranges were like nothing I had ever eaten before. They were beyond delicious. They were very juicy and so sweet. Nothing back home even compared to this quality of fruit. I was sad when we ran out of them, and they didn't last long.

Sarge had his own agendas. He had about two weeks before he had to report to base camp. So, he was off sightseeing and doing basically other boring shit. Jon and I had some wild oats to sew, so our itinerary was much more of the "How do we get cool and hip down here in hippie and surfer land!" Most of the shop owners and people on the street were cool. We started having breakfast at this little Balboa Café. A huge guy owned the joint, and he seemed very accommodating.

Jon and I made it a point to call Gary and leave a message at Pendleton that we were definitely in the neighborhood. We gave him the number of the Inn and hoped to see him soon. Inside, we knew that this could be the very last fling for the Golden Bears who bravely crossed the entire country, endured the charisma of 66, the hardships, the bullshit of criminals and now were ready to launch into a life of carefree living. Our first challenge and this was portrayed well in the movie 'The Endless Summer' was the 'Wedge' located at the southern tip of Balboa beach. It was time to get wet and wild and check out this body surfing action.

When you first see The Wedge, hear the thunder of the waves and see sheer wave height, you realize that this just might be way beyond any water experience that you have ever had. The beach was crowded and the waves that erupt along this pier section of ocean are impressive. They come in groups of three. Swimmers line the water, mostly out where the waves start to build and wait for the perfect wave. You need at least one swim fin and a lot of guys to do this. There were people in wheelchairs all over the beach, and most of them had signs on the back of their chairs that read 'Victim of the Wedge'. Not real consoling when you're a newcomer from the Midwest and the biggest wave you've seen has been on Lake Erie.

The two biggest things that I learned that day was, when someone flashed two fingers at you in a V formation, it meant 'Peace', and the word 'bitching' basically means 'cool' or 'okay'. Otherwise, the other lesson learned was to become a spectator at The Wedge and just look like you're riding a wave every so often. The pounding that you get from 10 feet of water crashing down on your body and driving you into the sand is not pleasant. Jon had a good portion of his forehead ripped off when a giant wave crashed him headfirst into the sand. Then another wave finished off the job. He was lucky that his neck didn't snap. Then we would have been just as unlucky as the poor saps lining the beach in wheelchairs.

This injury, though, had a silver lining to it. We got hooked up with some real beach ladies who took care of Jon, dressed his wound, and offered us food, wine, and companionship. Plus, they were cute. The best of the bunch and the leader of the group was 'Tookie'. She was a tall blonde, well-tanned, and had that Paris Hilton look. She drove a Woodie and seemed to be able to come and go as she pleased. She was definitely into her image, because I can't remember her ever going into the water. The surfboards on the top of her Woodie seemed to have been strapped there long ago. Tookie seemed to be quite attracted to Jon. He was quite a superstar; tall, dark, muscular, and tan. He kinda had that Steve Reeves look going for him, with a low voice. He was also well hung.

The Wedge incident had burned most of his forehead skin off. It was like a very serious rug burn. Tookie came to our beach house, applied ointment to Jon's forehead, and then she'd hang around for the rest of the day. She definitely added to the California beach bum scene. It was hard not to stare at her body because she always had a bikini on. She had a smile to die for, a thin waist, totally tan, and piercing blue eyes. It didn't take long, probably less than 24 hours before Jon had her in the outside, playing volleyball and drinking Coors in 7 oz. cans. Sarge was still gone, off doing his tourist thing. So, we had the run of our three-room bungalow.

Gary showed up one night while he was on a weekend furlough. He immediately rented another bungalow next to ours, and on the other side, a lady who seemed to be in her middle to late twenties. Gary and I got really involved in the evening activities with the rest of the beach community while

Jon milked his injuries for sympathy so that Tookie would take care of and fuck him.

Gary wasn't really interested in hustling any beach girls. It was obvious in his swagger, his talk, and general mannerisms that the Marines had molded him into a kill-ready grunt. He shared with us that he'd been fucking so many prostitutes down in Mexico while on furloughs that he wasn't looking for any relationships. One night, Jon and Tookie were in Gary's beach house, and I was over getting ready to sleep at Sarge's place. There was a large double-bed that came out of the wall in the main room, and that's where I was crashing. All of a sudden, in through the front door came Tookie. She was obviously pissed off about something. "That damn Jon!" And with that, I kind of muttered, "Fine."

Tookie turned on a bedside table lamp and then took off her bikini. She turned, and while standing there totally nude, she started pulling up the sheets and fluffing the pillow. What a body! Damn. Small tits, with soft rounded nipples. Her stomach was ribbed and tapered down to a slim waist. Her pussy was covered with very light-blonde hair, and as she crawled into bed, her long hair dangled over her chest, and it just made for a perfect sensual sight. As she laid down, she rolled over so as to face away from me. She thanked me for being so generous, and then we both went to sleep.

However, I stared at her naked back, waist, and butt for a while before I could relax enough to sleep. She was the consummate California beach bunny. I thought to myself, *this is why we came to California.* We wanted to spread our wings and our experiences, and we've done that. These were the beginning days of the so-called sexual revolution, and we're actors right in the middle of this huge plot going on in society. The war, the civil unrest, the busting out of the Golden Bear bubble, and the realization that we can do as we please made it hard to decide whether to cry or rejoice. Our nation was going to shit, and we were basically experiencing unbridled hedonism. What a life! How long we could make it last was the unspoken question.

As the days and weeks passed, Gary would show up on Friday nights, and we'd hang out with the locals. We'd play beach volleyball, have a bonfire, and drink Coors until late at night. I finally made a connection with the twenty-year-old chick who lived next to the bungalow that Gary rented. Believe it or not, her last name was Pleasant, and she was. The more I got to know her, the more I was attracted to her. One night, following the bonfire, she invited me into her beach house. We literally sat on the bed all night long, talking about life and its many tribulations. She had grown up on an Indian reservation in Oklahoma and had lived a very conservative life. She never went to college, and she knew very little about big city life, relationships, geography or much of anything outside life on the reservation. Miss Pleasant was just that, a cool person, soft, enjoyable, and she had a killer body. One thing that I found out from her was that she had never had a steady boyfriend, and lo and behold she was a virgin, or so she claimed!

Damn! The next morning, once the sun came up and Jon had gotten out of bed, I just had to share that with him. "Bullshit!" was his remark. "She's just bullshitting you!" Well, later that night, it was as though history was repeating itself. Miss Pleasant and I ended up at her place after the volleyball game was over, and we just talked. However, our talk now was more about relationships and the birds and the bees. We sat very close together on her bed, and I massaged her leg as we talked, and I stared deep into her eyes. Man, she was cute, and her body was nice. She was thin, about 5'4", blue eyes and long hair that she wore in an up fashion. I doubt if she had ever had a haircut.

Well, long into our chat, she gets up and goes to her bathroom. I figured that she had to pee since we'd drank about 12 mini-Coors. When she returned, she had on a very short bathrobe. She sat back down very close to me. I couldn't resist the urge anymore, so I leaned over and kissed her. It was like kissing a girl in the 6th grade. Then she looks at me and says, "Will it hurt?" I replied, "Will what hurt?" "Will it hurt if you have intercourse with me?" I was like getting stage fright now. Holy crap, this physically mature, good-looking, full-blown lady is asking me if I'm going to hurt her if I pop her cherry. Wow! An opportunity like this doesn't happen every day. As a matter of fact, I doubt if many guys ever have this kind of experience.

I reassured her that if she'd let me, there would only be enjoyment. We proceeded to kiss, and soon, she was really starting to warm up to the experience. Our tongues intertwined, and as I untied her belt on her robe, underneath was a warm, very white, luscious body. Her nipples were hard and erect, her stomach was flat and tight, and when I made my way down to her pussy with my hand, she was very tight. Her pussy was wet and responsive. I stroked her clit after wetting it with my spit. She immediately started to jump as I stroked her. She was gushing fluids and she even started to moan. I knelt above her and gazed at her gorgeous body as her blue eyes stared at me. I removed my shirt and my jean cut-offs. I placed her hand on my cock and held it as I showed her how to stroke it ever so softly and slowly. Then I laid back down next to her and as she jacked me off, I continued to stroke her clit, finger her pussy and kiss her nipples. Miss Pleasant was getting so excited that it was evident that she was going to orgasm.

She was about ready to jump out of the bed she was thrusting so hard and moaning so deeply, then she finally came. Her body just became limp. I then rolled over on top of her and spit into my hand and lubricated the end of my cock. I spread her legs and tried to softly and slowly enter her hot pussy without too much disruption to her enjoyment. Well, my penis made it about one half in, and then it was just too thick to go any further without rupturing her vagina, or so I thought. So, I just stroked her with half a cock and continued to lick, kiss, and suck her nipples and breasts. As I came, the increased lubrication allowed me to slide in a bit further, but I thought that no way did I want to traumatize this lady. I wanted her again, now, tonight, and for who knows how long.

Gary showed up the following day, which was exciting each time he visited. It was like old times, and we were still just kids. We weren't old enough to vote, drink, or buy a house via a mortgage. We sure as hell were old enough to become soldiers and go kill people or be killed. It sure didn't make any sense, but so much of what was going on in the States and the world didn't make any sense. So, tuning out and turning on was an emerging national creed among the young generation that was easy to subscribe to. I shared with Gary my experience with Miss Pleasant. He looked at me with a lot of doubt, but he then seemed to believe what I was telling him about her being as pure as the driven snow.

Later that night after the bonfire, Gary and I wanted to watch TV. We didn't have one in our bungalow, but Miss Pleasant did have one. She worked two jobs on the weekends, and she never got home until the wee hours of the morning. She had left her kitchen window unlocked and had told me that if I ever wanted to use her place to sleep, eat or watch TV, that it was fine. Just come in through the window. Well, that's what Gary and I did. Jon and Tookie were off somewhere, and none of us had seen Sarge in quite a while. The next day, Gary and I were outside in the courtyard working on the Abalone shells, and the building manager, a British guy who was usually cool, came up to us and said, "What were you guys doing breaking into bungalow number 9 last night?" "Hey!" I responded. "I have permission to enter Miss Pleasant's place anytime I want. She told me I could, and she even leaves the window open, so I don't need a key." He looked at me and said, "Well, that arrangement is over. I've had complaints about this. Plus, I asked Pleasant if she knew anything about this and she said, 'No!'" Bullshit!

Well as fate would have it, for some strange reason I didn't see Pleasant anywhere for a while. I caught her leaving her place one morning for work and tried to stop and talk with her, and she treated me as if I was a stranger. No wonder she never had any lovers! I think that this lady may have had a screw loose, or she was screwed up by being screwed, or I didn't use and abuse her to her level of satisfaction, so I was a failure in her eyes. Who knows? She became history really quickly.

Sarge showed up finally and to a point we were starting to get worried about him. He had a tall, mid-twenties, blonde dude with him who he said that he met in a bar down in Tijuana Mexico. We moved over to Gary's bungalow, and Sarge had Denny staying at his place. One day, Jon and I went down to the local sport shop in Newport and purchased a snorkel, diving mask, fins and a three-banded speargun with two arrows, and a large, barbed pointed blade. We had seen a great white shark that was hauled up on the dock by the fishing boat for the Bal-Broaster and the captain told us that he had been regularly seeing great whites while they were out netting. Damn! The one on the dock was so large that I think I could have crawled down its throat. Neither of us had ever seen anything like this.

Later that night, at the bonfire, as we all sat around drinking Coors, Jon shared with one of the cool guy locals what we had purchased. Well, it was his hobby to dive for Abalone. Jon had quite a bit of diving experience, and he could hold his breath longer than anyone I had ever known, so he and this dude talked for hours. It was suggested that we get a truck innertube and put a net in the middle of it. Abalone are found in deeper water, so you need a place to store them after you've collected them. The guy steered us to a place right below Harry Bellefonte's house that was high up on a cliff overlooking the ocean. He had told Jon that this was a large kelp bed and that it was full of fish and shell creatures. He also said that he had seen an occasional shark out there.

I think that we were headed to marina Del Ray the next morning. Tookie's Woodie was perfect for the job. She was going to sunbathe as we swam our way out into this vast can of spinach to find the ultimate cash crop. Abalone!

We were out about one quarter of a mile and to me that was far enough. The water looked very dark and deep. I had the speargun, which was not cocked, with me up at the tube and Jon suited up with the mask, fins and snorkel, plus a prying knife and headed for the bottom. He was gone for quite a while and then he resurfaced and exclaimed, "Damn, There's a lot of vegetation down there. Shit, there's fish everywhere but it's awful deep to make it to the bottom." Jon persisted and went down again. All of a sudden, he came splashing to the surface and had his arms spread apart. He raised his mask and yelled, "Damn, I'm not sure what I just swam up to but it is large, very large."

And with that, a huge balloon of bubbles surfaced behind Jon, and he started swimming toward me. Well, it might as well have been a movie because what was coming, I guess, could have been expected. We were two diving virgins, and so here comes the biggest cock in the ocean. You know it's true. Great white sharks do swim with their dorsal fin out of the water, and I was looking directly at one as it circled us about seventy-five yards out. I never thought that my mouth could get dry sitting in the largest body of water on the planet, but it was. Frankly, I could hardly talk. Getting eaten was not on my agenda for the day.

Well, just as quickly as that giant behemoth surfaced, it disappeared. However, you could watch the kelp tops move as the giant predator swam around us. It would then dive, we'd wait, and then it would surface again. Shit! I was outta here. Jon swam toward me and grabbed the un-cocked spear gun. "I thought that you loaded this thing."

"What, you want to shoot that creature with the spear? That's only going to piss it off and fill the water with blood," I exclaimed. It was now time to do what every brave man would do. Swim for shore and don't look back! That damn fish took another swipe at us, and it was much closer than the first circle it made. Fuck this! I'm headed to shore. So, I grabbed the tube and swam as fast as I humanly could. About every 10 feet, I'd get hit with a big clump of kelp, and it almost made me shit my pants because I thought that monster had a hold of me.

Jon was still out in the deep, trying to cock the gun, but it was just too difficult to do without some sort of brace behind him. So, he too took the 'let's save our ass' way out. He headed toward shore, too. I really don't think that I was ever more scared in my life. By the time I got to shore, I was so panicked and out of breath that I seriously thought my heart was going to stop. Tookie had come town to the seashore because she could see the great white from up in the dunes. "You guys are lucky to be alive! Those bastards start coming in here in the fall because of the warmer water and tons of bait fish. Thank you, Jacques Cousteau, for that moment in Marine time facts. Fuck! We almost became food." Jon was rather pissed when he came rolling in with the waves.

"Hell, why did you leave so quickly? I wanted to shoot that bastard." We never did settle on the size of that bastard but we both agreed that it was bigger than the two of us. Hell, its head was bigger than me and at that time I weighed about 180 lbs. and was 5'9". Jon was 6 ft. tall, 210 lbs. and we looked like minnows. This was like Moby Dick with a taste for humans. Regardless, it was not Abalone!

The Times, They Are A-Changing

Fall was upon us, and Gary started to warn us that he would soon be shipped out to Vietnam. Jon and I were getting restless to continue our journey and head north to San Francisco. We wanted to do the Haight-Ashbury thing and check out the free-love movement. Sarge and Denny were as thick as thieves, and Sarge, too, knew it was getting near the time for him to return to base.

One Friday night, there was a lot of Ode to Summer celebrating going on in the town. Sarge and Denny went looking for parties to crash, and Jon, Tookie, Gary, and I, plus a few other beach girls sat around the bonfire, drinking Coors and telling stories. I finally reached my maximum and headed to bed. It started to get pretty chilly outside, so they moved the gathering into our beach house.

Soon, Sarge and Denny came back with a tale of getting pushed around at a party because they were stealing food out of this apartment's refrigerator. Denny was louder than hell and trying to fire everyone up to go kick these guy's asses. He woke me up and I had heard part of his story, and I made some comment like "Well you probably deserved it." Blam! This asshole jumps on top of me and starts pounding me in the head. I just got up the adrenaline so that I could roll over and knock his tall ass to the floor, then Jon, Sarge, and Gary all tackled him and took him outside. Man did my head hurt. I went back to bed, Tookie brought me some ice for my head, and those guys all headed over to this apartment where this happened. I didn't get the full story until the next morning, but Sarge and Denny were in jail, and Gary and Jon more or less stayed out of the mix.

By mid-morning Denny, and get this, his mother showed up at Sarge's place. I guess that she bailed his ass out of jail. He was missing several front teeth and immediately, he starts jumping into my shit as to why I wasn't helping him. Again, I said, "You probably deserved your beating, and going to jail is a good thing for you." With that, the asshole tried coming after me. Great,

I put a clamp hold on his neck that would have killed a cobra. Jon and Gary grabbed him and told him to get the hell out of there with his mommy! So, off he went with him needing to say the last word, "This is not settled between us. I'll see you again."

"Fuck off," was my response. Sarge was next, and he too showed up with his mother. He had a black eye, and he was pretty reserved. He told us that we were free to continue to stay in the bungalow until the end of the following week. He was off to base to get ready to head back to Vietnam. We exchanged addresses and phone numbers and then off he went. He was a nice guy, but as the years would go by, we never heard from him.

Gary continued for about one more week to show on weekends, but he shared with us that it was time for him to say *hasta la vista*, and he was off to Vietnam. Our British landlord told Jon and I that it was time that we vacated Sarge's place because he had checked out. He wasn't open to the notion that Sarge had prepaid our continued stay. Gary's rent was only paid through the weekend, so Jon and I prepared to head north and visit the surfing championships in Huntington Beach and check out a rock concert in Sacramento that featured Janis Joplin, Big Brother and Holding Company and Jefferson Airplane. Then we wanted to do Frisco and the Napa Valley. After that, our plans were unclear.

We both knew that our journey was going to end soon, and we'd both be headed back to reality. Probably back to the care and supervision of our parents. Tookie vanished, and she took the beach girl image with her. I don't think that Jon ever even knew her last name. Too bad, because she was one heck of a little lady, but she was caught up in her own little niche, much like those who were Golden Bears. She lived within the parameters of certain unwritten rules that set limits on what she could or could not do. To continue to be an icon on this little peninsula, she had to retreat.

Here we were, Jon, Gary, and I, together for possibly the very last time. This was the end of our teen years. We had grown up as Golden Bears, partied as Golden Bears, and thrived in the Golden Bear society, even though we very often just did as we pleased. We really didn't know better. At one time, we were under the delusion that these were the best years of our lives and the best of times, but we had now learned that life was just beginning, and for many, their Golden Bear experience was miserable, and for a few, it was the only thing they had going on. Sad, because we were learning that there is a hell of a lot more to life outside the bubble, however much of it is ugly.

It all started with friendships back in elementary school, the gift of a baseball bat, and many years of everyday friendship. There was trust and loyalty among us that far transcended just being CROs together. We were friends through thick and thin, and now it was time to separate and go out various ways. I knew that Gary would give anything to accompany us on our journey north to stay with the popular culture to ride the wave of the anti-establishment movement just have more fun, laughs, love and experiences with those who he knew best. That wasn't going to happen. He was committed to his Marine Corps duties, and even though he loved the wild side of life, he was dedicated to going to fight an enemy that he had never read about, knew about or even met.

Jon and I got Gary's stuff organized, and we arranged a ride down the Pendleton with a local named Del to send him off properly. We stopped at a couple of beaches along the way in Del's VW, just to enjoy the view, sip a few micro-Coors, and look at the beach bunnies. However, they were becoming few in number. The sea was starting to cool, and the beach crowd was moving indoors. We even went and visited President Nixon's California home before going to the base. We all wanted to see where 'tricky dick' lived.

My grandmother, who was staunchly Catholic, very holy and probably someday a saint, always said that he was evil. Maybe he was, who knows. He certainly wasn't respected by the younger generation. Dropping Gary off and saying goodbye was without fanfare. It hurt. We tried to keep it on the up and up, but it still hurt. We all knew too well of what was waiting for him on the other side of the Pacific, in a country that none of us or our relatives had ever visited. A place where you had to look on a map to find out where it was and it was the 'killing fields' of so many of our friend's older brothers and sisters, plus many of our friends too. We said our goodbyes, unloaded Gary's things, and wished him good luck. Then, off we went, back north. Del wanted us to return to Newport, but Jon and I had other ideas. So, we had him pick up our traveling gear and drop us off on Highway 1. North was our compass point for continued adventure! For the second time in our short lives, I had to say, "Goodbye."

"Wow! Seriously, wow! Dang, WTF, you highly entitled types are rather moral less, genital focused creeps. However, your stories are very entertaining," exclaimed TAZ. "And am I to assume that your high times at Ridgemont High School was kind of a precursor to the free-love era?"

"Well, now thinking through this unique journey, time to reach out to a few peeps and see what's up," I added. It's going to be interesting to find out who's still standing and who even remembers me. Although far too often, I was the proverbial loudest in the room of life. "No doubt!" TAZ expressed with a grin.

"So, Mr. Mental health professional, community organizer, prevention program and child advocacy expert plus musician has a huge backstory. Again, wow! You should publish a Shades of Grey for Teens," TAZ injected with a lot of sarcasm.

"No doubt! My bad! I literally have been praying for forgiveness for a very long time. Plus, my professional life reflects me advising on the many good choices I should have made. How my growing up, experiences, friendships and so much more has literally now enlightened me to all of the unique qualities in life," I shared with a look of trust. TAZ just smiled. "So, what now?" TAZ tossed out. "Well, moving forward, peeps to the lodge. A small gathering of CROs to just get re-aligned."

"What, no ORCs?" TAZ shouted.

"No, this will be a guy thang," I responded. "I am going to go back in time. I will review photos from Tremont Elementary, St. Agatha, Watterson, and Upper Arlington. Plus, I will look at what few photos I have from past reunions. Out of all that, I will go to the UAHS website and try to narrow down a short list of who to send an invitation. Six, but no more than eight."

"Again, Loverboy, WTF? You have a circular staircase to your loft. Best advice is to find out what handicap accommodations are needed," TAZ offered up with a tone of sarcasm. "Let me remind you that you have a huge black-and-white photo of your high school graduating class in the barn. That should be perfect for developing your invite list."

"Great idea! I forgot about that. So, I should be able to uncover a proverbial hit list if I dig deep enough," I added.

So now, another leg of this life's journey rises from the ashes of one's memory. Certainly, many have been lost along the way and that too, becomes part of our story. One thing is for certain, CRO '67 will live on.

Our reunions were planned years ago to go until we are 80 years old…WTF!

To be continued…possibly many times!

UTES
UTES
UTES

ST. AGATHA SCHOOL
FIRST HOLY COMMUNION

N.I.H.S. Class of 1967 Reunion

Upper Arlington High - 1967

ST. AGATHA SCHOOL
COLUMBUS, OHIO
GRADE 6   1960-61
Alston Studios, Inc.

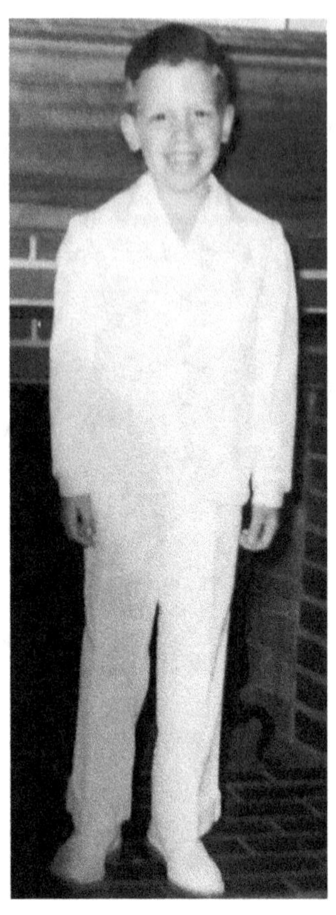